# Global Mobile

CONNECTING WITHOUT WALLS, WIRES, OR BORDERS

Fred Johnson

Peachpit
Press

## Global Mobile

CONNECTING WITHOUT WALLS, WIRES, OR BORDERS

Fred Johnson

### Peachpit Press

1249 Eighth Street
Berkeley, CA 94710
510/524-2178
800/283-9444
510/524-2221 (fax)

Find us on the World Wide Web at: www.peachpit.com
To report errors, please send a note to errata@peachpit.com

Peachpit Press is a division of Pearson Education
Copyright © 2005 by Frederick V. Johnson

Developmental Editor: Cary Norsworthy
Production Editor: Hilal Sala
Copyeditor: Corbin Collins
Technical Editor: Owen Linzmayer
Compositor: Maureen Forys, Happenstance Type-O-Rama
Indexer: Joy Dean Lee
Cover design: Charlene Will
Cover illustration: Fred Johnson
Contributing writer: Owen Linzmayer
Interior design: Mimi Heft with Maureen Forys
Photos: Fred Johnson

ISBN 0-321-27871-2

9 8 7 6 5 4 3 2 1

Printed and bound in the United States of America

## Dedication

This book is dedicated to *Alexis R. Johnson* and *Eric T. Johnson,* the best kids in the world.

And to:

*Thomas V. Johnson,* also known as "the rock." Dad, thanks for making and raising me.

*Sheryl Holman,* my sister and never-ending source of inspiration.

*Karen Dingle,* my other sister, who doesn't realize how amazing she really is.

*Daryl V. Johnson,* my brother whom I always wished I could be more like.

*Thomas V. Johnson, Jr.,* my other brother who always gave me priceless advice during our bunk-bed counseling sessions.

I'd also like to thank the beautiful *Elsa Geremew,* for putting up with (among other things) my absence, both mentally and physically, during this project.

And last but not least—*Ruth Johnson,* my mother. Ma, I really wish you were around to hold this book in your hands…but I know you were with me when I was writing it.

## Acknowledgments

My sincerest thanks go out to:

*Cary Norsworthy,* the bestest editor a guy could have. Cary, thank you for your amazing blend of professionalism, humor, and flexibility. Without you this book would not exist.

*Nancy Aldrich-Ruenzel,* for having faith in me and allowing this project to happen.

*Scott Cowlin,* for being the conduit that made this book possible, and for his subsequent marketing prowess.

*Marjorie Baer,* for being a never-ending source of inspiration and tolerance. Marjorie, thank you for helping me crack the dreaded writer's block.

*Owen Linzmayer,* for writing the cell phone chapter, and for painstakingly tech reviewing the other chapters. Also, *Eric Levine* and *John R. Chang* for their contributions to the cell phone chapter.

*Corbin Collins,* for flawlessly copyediting this book, and making it appear that I really have mastered the English language.

*Mimi Heft* and *Maureen Forys,* for the unique design of the pages in this book. You've made this book as much of a pleasure to look at as I hope it is to read.

*Hilal Sala,* for shepherding this book's production, and helping turn a discombobulated folder full of Microsoft Word files into something useful.

*Joy Dean Lee,* for your painstaking work in compiling all of the arcane acronyms in this book into an indispensable index.

*Charlene Will,* for allowing me to create the cover art for this book— and for your guidance in helping me design a piece that I hope people will like—and for the flawless typesetting of the final cover.

*Jim Heid,* for extending his wonderful reality-distortion field around me, helping me believe I could actually do this… Jim! Look! I DID IT!

# Table of Contents

# Introduction

*Today's mobile professional has many more communication options than were available just a few short years ago. Advances in portable computing, wireless technology (Wi-Fi), telephone technology, and networks have made mobile life easier and more exciting. But with so many choices, selecting the right gear and services is also more challenging.*

# What This Book is About

When you get right down to it, just about any portable computer or cell phone will do the job for most *Global Mobile* travelers. Even entry-level models of these devices are usually more than you really need to send the occasional email or make a simple phone call. But then, you're not really the entry-level kind of user, are you? You probably opted for one of the better laptops available at the time and a cell phone that probably has enough bells and whistles to keep you entertained for hours—and you probably haven't even scratched the surface of what superpowers you have available to you.

This book is about helping you explore the powers you probably already have and making the right choices to expand them. Essentially, it is a book about connecting the dots. In this case, the dots are your laptop computer, your cell phone, and wireless and Ethernet broadband network connections. Let's face it, you're a busy professional and you don't have time to *geek-out*. That's where this book comes in.

*Global Mobile* doesn't try to educate you on nuances of the various technologies you have in your possession—rather it educates you on how to get them up and running in the quickest way possible. For example, you've heard you can connect to these Wi-Fi hotspots, and assume it's probably easy…and it is. But you've never actually done it. This book will take you through the steps, tell you what to expect, and have you connected in no time.

I take a "day in the life" approach to explaining things. You'll learn what you should be thinking about before you even start packing your suitcase all the way through to when you've finally arrived at your destination. But I don't stop there; you also get the low-down on Wi-Fi: what it is, what it can do for you, and where it's probably going. *Bluetooth* may be a term you've heard quite a bit lately; I explain what it is, what it isn't, and why it's a good thing.

## How to Use This Book

This book is not a shopping guide; you won't find many product comparisons or recommendations here (though I do point you to some convenient locations where you can buy gear). Instead, this book is a usage guide, designed to be kept with you in your laptop bag to help you through those sticky situations at a moment's notice. Simply flip to the chapter you need and you're on your way. Example? Say you're at the hotel and need to check your email, but this particular hotel doesn't have high-speed Internet access—only a stone-aged phone jack. Just flip to Chapter 3, follow the step-by-step instructions, and you'll be dialed up in no time. You'll even find a handy chart listing some of the more popular Internet Service Providers.

I've attempted to make this book conversational in tone—it's not meant to be a comprehensive manual of operation for your laptop or cell phone, but rather a knowledgeable friend who has agreed to help you be more productive.

But this book isn't only about connecting to the Internet in new and interesting ways; it's also about utilizing your cell phone, both domestically and abroad. One of the most confusing aspects (to some people, including me) about traveling with a mobile phone is how to dial out of one country and into another. This book helps you get your brain around the complexity of country codes, prefixes, and more. In the appendices you'll find helpful charts listing the country codes and dialing procedures for most of the inhabited countries on this planet. With this book, you won't waste time asking, "How do I dial out of this country?" In fact, people will probably start asking you.

Each chapter in this book is self-contained, meaning you can jump right to any chapter to learn about that particular facet of *Global Mobile* traveling.

## Chapter 1: Before You Go

It's all about planning—even Santa knows that to succeed, one has to make a list and check it twice. This chapter helps you think about and plan the various aspects of your upcoming trip. You'll learn how to choose a *Global Mobile*-friendly hotel, pick the correct power adapters, and use your cell phone at your destination (foreign or domestic). You'll even find a helpful packing list to help make sure you bring the necessary items.

## Chapter 2: In Transit

Once you've left home, you're pretty much on your own. Whatever you've packed is what you've got to work with until you get to your destination. In this chapter, I take you through the things you need to know in order to get and stay connected while at the airport (gate), sitting on the plane, and even when you've finally touched down and the flight attendant announces that you can once again make calls to the outside world.

## Chapter 3: At Your Destination

This chapter helps you make the most of your home away from home. Setting up this temporary home base doesn't have to be complicated. Get unpacked, plugged in, and logged on in no time. You'll also find some helpful tips for making the most of that expensive high-speed Internet connection by setting up a private wireless network that you and your traveling companions can all use.

### Chapter 4: Working While on the Road

After you've arrived at your destination and successfully connected to the Internet, it's time to get to work. This chapter will demystify some of the voodoo surrounding connecting to your corporate network while abroad. You'll learn what a VPN is and how to use it.

### Chapter 5: In Public Places

Whether you're at home or on the road, you'll probably find the need to connect to the Internet from someplace other than your home base. This chapter gives you instructions on how to find places that connect you, and also how to connect when you've found them. You'll also find some interesting tips on how to exchange files with other *Global Mobile* travelers, with or without a hotspot.

### Chapter 6: Text Messaging (SMS)

As technology advances, people have developed a need to get their ideas across faster than ever before. Text messaging allows near-instantaneous messages to be sent over networks. There are several tricks that allow you to do this efficiently, and in some cases for free. This chapter goes through the ins and outs of sending text messages; you'll also find a helpful chart of abbreviated words to help reduce the size of your messages and the calluses on your thumbs.

### Chapter 7: Getting Online with Your Cell Phone

There are times when you're away from home and have no access to Wi-Fi, broadband, or even a phone jack. That's where your cell phone comes in. You'll learn about how to use it with your laptop to get online, and you'll learn about Bluetooth, an up-and-coming technology that allows devices to connect to each other without the use of wires. You'll also learn some interesting ways that evil-doers are attempting to exploit this relatively fledgling technology.

## Chapter 8: Emerging Technologies

Technology moves at such a rapid pace, no book can ever hope to be completely up to date. The technologies I discuss in this book continue to evolve and offer users more and more interesting capabilities. In this chapter, you get a glimpse at where Wi-Fi, Bluetooth, and other technologies are headed.

Use this book as your always-with-you traveling companion. Keep it in your bag and refer to it whenever the need arises. Visit the *Global Mobile* Web site at www.fredjohnson.net/globalmobile/ for printable versions of some of the more useful charts in the book.

Happy travels!

# CHAPTER ONE

# Before You Go

*My dad used to tell me, "If you fail to plan, you might as well plan to fail." When I was in the Scouts, our motto was* Be prepared. *This advice is especially apt when traveling. For instance, having the latest wireless gear will do you no good if you can't recharge it. And what good is it to bring the latest cell phone if you can't make a call in the country that you're visiting? What about lugging your laptop halfway around the world only to find you can't figure out how to connect it to the Internet?*

Preparing for your trip doesn't have to be complicated. Start off by asking yourself a few questions:

- **Where am I going?**

  This is the first and most important question you can ask your-self. Of course you know where you're going, but in the context of getting and staying connected, your gear needs to know where it's going as well. For instance, you need to know what kind of voltage and power adapters you might need in your tar-get country, or you will find yourself disconnected and power-less very quickly.

- **How will I get there?**

  Depending on your mode of travel, you might have options that make your trip more pleasant and more "plugged in."

- **What will I do when I arrive?**

  Are you traveling for business or pleasure? What level of access do you want when you arrive? If you're flying to Cabo San Lucas to get away from civilization, you probably don't want civiliza-tion to have easy access to you. However, if you're flying on the company's dime to conduct business, you probably want to be as connected as possible (during the day at least). Thinking about these factors can help you decide what to take and what to leave safely at home.

Whether you're traveling for business or pleasure, there are some things you should plan in advance if you want to maintain some connection to home, colleagues, and of course the Internet.

After you make your plane reservations, the next thing you'll prob-ably do is find a place to stay. If you're on business, you'll ideally want to stay somewhere that offers a broadband Internet connec-tion—and even if you're not on business, at the very least you'll want an affordable dial-up Internet option. In either case, you probably want to use a cell phone and you'll need to make sure it works at your destination.

# Connecting to the Internet Away from Home

In the past, if you stayed at a reasonably well-known chain hotel, you could rest assured that your room would have at least some level of comfort. But that was before the Internet became part of our daily lives. Now you have additional concerns—can you connect to the 'net from your hotel?

### Broadband (aka—a fast Internet connection)

Don't assume that a hotel has broadband Internet access. When lining up your hotel, be sure to ask: "Do you have broadband Internet access *in* the rooms?"

Many hotels have business centers where you can get on the Internet, but laptops give you more flexibility: Do you want to use some stuffy public office when you could be emailing and surfing the Web in the comfort of your own room? If always-on broadband is important to you when you travel, and the hotel doesn't offer it in your room, thank them and move on to the next hotel on your list. There are lots of fish in the sea.

### Wi-Fi (aka—a wireless Internet connection)

If you want to kick it up a notch and really be flexible, consider staying at a hotel that offers wireless broadband access (Wi-Fi, short for Wireless Fidelity) to its guests. Wi-Fi is shorthand for the

---

## Major hotel chains that offer Wi-Fi

**Best Western** (Free in rooms and lobby)

**Hilton** (Free in lobby, broadband in rooms for a fee)

**Holiday Inn** (Free in rooms and lobby)

**Hotel Ibis** (Europe: Wi-Fi for a fee, check with individual locations)

**Marriott** ($2.95 per 15 minutes in lobby, broadband in rooms for a fee)

**Ramada** (No Wi-Fi, free broadband in rooms)

**W Hotel** (Free Wi-Fi in lobby, broadband in rooms for a fee)

802.11 wireless networking standard (or, as Intel calls it, Centrino technology). We'll be talking a lot more about wireless access later in the book, but for now suffice to say that if your hotel has it, you want it.

There is one catch to this, though (there's always a catch, isn't there?). You need to make sure your computer has the hardware and software to use that wireless network. Here is how to find out if you're part of the Wi-Fi elite:

### Mac

If you're using an Apple Macintosh portable computer that you purchased (new) within the last 2 to 3 years, chances are you already have AirPort installed. If you don't have it, you can easily buy and install an AirPort Card. AirPort is Apple's brand name for its wireless capability, which is really just another name for the same 802.11 Wi-Fi wireless standard.

### PC

Some PC laptops marked "Intel Inside" might also display a Centrino logo. If your computer has no visible indicator, take a peek at the Windows taskbar—the bar that runs along the bottom of the Windows XP screen with the Start button on the left. Within that bar, usually on the right side, is what Microsoft calls the Notification area, a dashboard of sorts that displays icons for programs currently running. If you've got wireless networking installed, you'll probably see an icon that looks something like the one on the right. Otherwise you can check in the system network configuration to see if there is an adapter present. Do this by navigating to Start > Control Panel > Network and Internet Connections > Network Connections. Double-click the Network Connections icon . It should indicate whether you've got wireless networking installed (for example, in the illustration I've got

*Wireless Networking icon*

*The Network Connections icon*

a WaveLAN card installed), or if you're merely Ethernet (wired networking) enabled.

In either case, if you do not have a wireless adapter installed in your computer, you can purchase one from most major computer retailers for around $100 U.S. They're fairly easy to configure, but configuration varies from manufacturer to manufacturer, so check the manual.

*Network Connections lets you view all your connection options. Your wireless capability would be displayed here.*

## Dial-up (your last resort)

*Be sure that the plug that you connect to at the hotel is an analog plug! Data ports on hotel phones are almost always analog, but—before you plug into a wall jack— check with the hotel's front desk to make sure it's not a digital jack, or you can ruin your computer—and your trip.*

If you don't have broadband Internet access in your room, then you'll need to use "narrowband," which means plugging into an analog phone jack and using a good old-fashioned modem (remember those?) to connect. Or you'll have to dial up using your mobile phone and connect your laptop to it with either a wired connection (usually a USB cable between your phone and computer) or a wireless (Bluetooth) connection. We'll be digging deeper into the mysteries of Bluetooth in Chapter 7; for now, just know that Bluetooth is a technology that lets you replace wires with, well, wireless.

Before you leave, you'll also need to bring or find a local or toll-free phone number to your ISP (Internet Service Provider) or your company's server in order to connect. If your ISP doesn't have a local number where you are, you'll be incurring long-distance or international phone charges each time you access the Internet, plus any additional dial-up, toll-free, and roaming charges that may be added onto your service. For example, as of this writing, the ISP Earthlink offers local dial-up numbers in many European countries, but it also charges its members an additional $9 per hour roaming fee. Regardless of whether you connect with a local number or an international one, connecting on a modem (even at the theoretical maximum of 56 Kbps) is slllooowww. Its snail's pace downloading speed only exacerbates the issue of paying additional phone rates just to do email.

## Connection gear

To use broadband, you'll need an Ethernet cable. To use dial-up, you'll need a telephone cable. The U.S. standard phone jack is called RJ11. It's becoming more of an international standard, although many countries use phone cables that look like a U.S. connection on one end (which goes into your laptop or into the phone set) but use a totally different connection on the other end. Bring a U.S. cable with you anyway, in case you have a modem port in your hotel telephone. If you don't, it might be difficult to find an adapter at the local hardware store—there are still some countries that haven't converted to the RJ11 plug type. In addition, some hotels have phones that are hard-wired directly into the wall with no jack connection at all. In that case, you should consider heading out of your hotel to an Internet café or Wi-Fi hotspot. And finally, don't forget to bring a power cord with the appropriate plug adapter for your destination country! See page 17 for examples of some of the commonly used plugs around the world.

*Use a straight-through (not cross-over) Category 5 Ethernet cable with RJ45 connectors on both ends.*

*An Ethernet cable (left) with an RJ45 connector, and an RJ11 phone jack (right)*

# Using a Cell Phone Internationally

Will you want to use your mobile phone while you're traveling? Probably. But you'll need to prepare before getting on the plane. There are a few issues you'll need to consider, such as what country you're traveling to, which carrier you're using, what kind of phone you have, whether it has a SIM (Subscriber Identity Module) card, and whether there are any potential security issues to worry about.

## Differences among countries

If you're an American traveling to Europe, you'll find that staying connected via your mobile phone is easier if you have a GSM (Global System for Mobile) phone. Those already using a GSM-based provider—such as T-Mobile or AT&T—need to have a three-band GSM telephone. The same is true if you live in Europe and you're traveling to the U.S., because there is more than one flavor of GSM—in fact it gets very complicated very quickly when you start looking at which countries use which frequencies. As a rule of thumb, North America and Central America are on GSM 1900 MHz, while most of the rest of the world is either on 900 or 1800 MHz or a combination of both. There is a list of all countries and their related GSM frequencies in Appendix A.

Traveling to Japan often means you should plan on renting a mobile phone that works with their 3G system or else be somewhat disconnected. (Japan is not on the GSM 900, 1800, or 1900 systems.) The problem with relying on Japanese local phones is that the instructions are in Japanese—unless you're able to read kanji, it's quite a puzzle trying to figure things out, not to mention the fact that the network operators and voicemail prompts are all in Japanese.

Fortunately, all is not lost—if you're a Vodafone customer, anyway. Vodafone has extended its network and roaming agreements into Japan. For Europeans currently using Vodafone as your carrier, it's a simple matter of renting a 3G phone in Japan and inserting your Vodafone SIM card into it. Of course, as I said before, you will be charged international roaming fees. But hey, you'll be connected, and you'll be using your own phone number…in Japan!

For Americans with Sprint PCS, you won't be able to make calls using your phone outside of the United States. In fact, the last time you'll be able to use your Sprint PCS phone is just before the flight attendant says, "Please turn off any unapproved electronic devices."

## Differences among carriers

Your carrier may or may not have international roaming agreements with the local carriers in other countries. Or it might be using a network that does not permit international roaming (for example, CDMA—see the chart on page 11). A week or more before you fly, call your carrier and inquire about its international service plans and roaming agreements. This short phone call could save you hundreds of dollars in roaming and long-distance fees.

## GSM and rental phones

If you have a three-band GSM phone that works on GSM 900/1800/1900 networks, you're already able to travel to many other countries with your own phone and your own telephone number. If you don't have a GSM phone that works outside your country, then you'll need to rent a mobile phone either before you leave or when you arrive in your destination country. Lots of companies offer international phone rentals—some of the better-known ones are Telestial, Inc. (www.telestial.com) and Cellular Abroad (www.cellularabroad.com).

## Swapping SIM cards

The next thing to consider is whether or not your phone has SIM capability. A SIM card is a little microchip that contains all the information

*For intrepid readers who want more information on how to use Japanese payphones, see www.yesjapan.com/culture*

*This is what a typical SIM card looks like, and is roughly the actual size.*

(account information, codes, and so on) that your phone needs to make and receive calls. The beauty of the SIM card is that it is tiny—roughly the size of your thumbnail—and it is removable. In many countries, you can buy a second SIM card from a local carrier and use it while you're traveling to make local calls without incurring local or international charges. Using a "rented" SIM will give you a local phone number, but bear in mind that anyone calling you from the U.S. will incur international calling rates instead of the domestic rate they incur when calling your U.S.-based number. And don't lose your original SIM card! However, before you can use another SIM card in your phone, you need to contact your provider for instructions on unlocking your phone.

## Unlocking your phone

The way cell phone service works is that the electronic serial number (ESN) in your phone acts like a digital fingerprint—it identifies you to your carrier and tells it what phone you're using. With the ESN, the carrier

---

### Buying a SIM card

When you arrive in your destination country, you might be able to buy a local SIM card in a telecom shop. What you want is a "pay-as-you-go" plan and not a month-to-month plan. These plans are offered by such international carriers as T-Mobile, Virgin Mobile, Vodafone, and Orange. You'll pay a flat fee for your card—this purchase typically includes your local phone number, a few minutes of air time, a voicemail box, and text messaging. After you use your start-up time, you can continue buying bulk minutes of air time that enable you to use your phone like a wireless phone card, while still being able to use the features that are built into your personal phone.

If you're concerned about finding a SIM card at your destination, you can also buy one (or even an unlocked GSM phone) before you leave—try some online services such as www.telestial.com or www.cellularabroad.com. Both of these companies sell SIM cards for a variety of countries (including the local voicemail features) and they offer a wealth of travel tips, as well.

can determine that your phone's serial number is in fact your phone and therefore knows to send calls to it when someone dials your number.

By contrast, a GSM phone is not directly linked to you. Instead, its SIM contains the unique ESN, and so the SIM identifies you to the wireless provider. The really cool thing about this is that you can put your SIM into most compatible GSM phones, because pretty much all current GSM phones are compatible with all current SIMs. Separating SIM circuitry from the phone hardware makes all sorts of things possible. Your wireless carrier doesn't give a hoot if you've changed phones—all it cares about is where to find your SIM. Your phone and SIM card are like a car and driver: The car is merely an empty shell without a driver, waiting to go somewhere. Slip a driver into that car, and suddenly transportation becomes possible. The same is true with SIMs and phones—slip that card into a phone, and suddenly you have communication power in your hands.

But there may be a catch: Many wireless providers *lock* their phones, meaning that their phones are programmed to work *only* with the SIMs issued by that company. Reversing that programming so that your phone can work with any SIM is called *unlocking*. Fortunately, as far as I know, all GSM phones can be unlocked.

If you're lucky, your phone can be unlocked by simply keying a secret code into it. The code is usually a unique number only for that particular phone, based on its serial number (called its IMEI, or International Mobile Equipment Identifier) coded by the service provider who locked it. Though the carrier probably won't unlock your phone for you, they will provide the code for you on request. Additionally, if you Google the phrase *unlocking a cell phone*, you might find instructions for unlocking your phone for free, as well as many companies that will do it for a fee.

Some types of phones need their *firmware* (operating system soft-ware) to be rewritten to remove the lock. This requires connecting the phone via a special data cable to a special programming unit.

## Communications standards

**GSM**—Global System for Mobile communications. Originally developed as a Europe-wide standard for digital mobile telephony, GSM has become the world's most widely used mobile system.

**GPRS**—The General Packet Radio Service is part of the GSM standard. It delivers "always-on" wireless packet data services to GSM customers. GPRS gives you data speeds of up to 115 Kbps. That's twice the speed of your 56 Kbps modem!

**TDMA**—Time Division Multiple Access is an advanced digital cellular platform that converts audio signals into a stream of digital information (made up of 1s and 0s). This is the same thing a modem does: It converts audio into easily transferable digital bits.

**CDMA**—Code Division Multiple Access. This technology was originally developed for military use over 30 years ago. Remember those humongous green brick-like walkie-talkies the soldiers used when they called in air strikes? They were using the same technology that Sprint PCS is using today.

**IDEN**—Integrated Digital Enhanced Network. A Motorola Inc. enhanced specialized mobile radio network technology that combines two-way radio, telephone, text messaging, and data transmission into one network.

**3G**—Third Generation. The term used to refer to the next generation of wireless communications technology, the first generation having been analog cellular, and the second generation being today's digital cellular networks.

**EDGE**—Enhanced Data Rates for GSM Evolution. The GSM service EDGE will increase the possible speed for transferring data to 384 Kbps.

**SIM**—A Subscriber Identity Module is a card commonly used in a GSM phone. The card holds a microchip that stores information and encrypts voice and data transmissions, making it close to impossible to listen in on calls. The SIM card also stores data that identifies the caller to the network service provider.

## Security issues

Treat your SIM card and your mobile phone as you treat your wallet or purse. Mobile phones are highly pilferable, valuable items. Keep your eyes on the prize.

If you happen to lose your SIM card, some bad guy (or girl) could potentially grab your card and begin making calls to anywhere on the planet, or—if they got their hands on your unlocked GSM phone, they could even toss your precious SIM card into the trash and pop in their own SIM card. If this happens, treat your lost SIM card just like a lost credit card. Call your mobile carrier immediately and let them know what happened. From that point forward, they will not allow any calls to be made from that particular SIM.

If you have a U.S. carrier and happen to be in the U.S. when you lose the card, you can walk into any of your carrier's retail outlets, get a new card, and immediately begin making calls again. If you're outside the U.S., then you'll probably have to "rent" a SIM card until you get back to the States.

# Trip Preparation

Here are the steps you'll need to take to ensure you'll be able to make phone calls when the plane lands:

- Before you leave, check with your carrier.

  Tell them you're going overseas and want the ability to make calls. Ask if they have any special international calling plans that you can sign up for. If they say their network doesn't support international roaming, you might need to rent a phone.

- If you're lucky enough to have a GSM carrier, make sure your phone has a SIM card.

You can easily find this out by checking your manual, and if you've tossed the manual just look under the battery. You won't need to disassemble your phone. If you have a phone that does not have a removable battery, it probably doesn't have a SIM card either (although some higher-end phones such as the Handspring Treo 600 don't have a removable battery, but do have a removable SIM card).

- Get a cheap, unlocked GSM phone with a SIM card.

  If you're on a GSM network, but don't have a phone that supports SIM cards, head to your carrier's retail outlet and pick up a cheap phone that has one. Most models manufactured in the last few years have this technology built in.

- Rent a phone.

  If you're on a mobile carrier that isn't using the GSM network, then you'll need to rent a phone (or use pay phones or phone cards). The charges will depend on the call usage and length of rental. Usually, if the daily calls average more than $10 U.S. per day, the rental is free. Otherwise, expect a rental charge of about $1.50 U.S. per day.

## Preparation by destination—some examples:

### TRAVEL TO EUROPE, CHINA, HONG KONG, SOUTH AMERICA

- Bring a GSM phone that works on GSM 900 and 1800 systems.

- Unlock your phone if you want to use a local SIM card.

- Bring plug adapters (for two- and three-prong devices) and an adapter for converting 220v to 110v.

- Make sure your laptop's power cable and your cell phone charger work on a 220-volt system.

*Americans traveling to countries that use 220v electricity need to "step down" the current to match their 110v appliances using a converter like the one shown here.*

**TRAVEL TO USA, CANADA, BERMUDA, BAHAMAS, MEXICO**

- Make sure your GSM phone is a three-band phone that works on GSM 1900 systems.

- Bring U.S. plug adapters and a voltage adapter (to convert electricity to 110v).

- Make sure your laptop's power cable and your cell phone charger work on a 110v system.

**TRAVEL TO JAPAN**

- Your cell phone might not work in Japan. You'll probably need to rent a Vodafone GSM 3G phone and check with your carrier to make sure it has a roaming agreement with Vodafone.

- Bring plug adapters that reduce three prongs to two.

- Consider a voltage adapter. Japan uses 100v versus the U.S. 110v. Many appliances work just fine when plugged into a Japanese outlet, but consider additional protection for sensitive appliances.

# Packing Checklist

| | |
|---|---|
| ☐ Laptop | ☐ Cell phone |
| ☐ Ethernet cable | ☐ Charger |
| ☐ Modem cable | ☐ Plug and voltage adapters |
| ☐ Power cord (AC) | ☐ Information on unlocking your phone |
| ☐ Plug and voltage adapters | ☐ International tech-support phone numbers |
| ☐ Wireless card | ☐ Rental information (if you don't have an international phone) |
| ☐ List of dial-up numbers | ☐ Extra battery (if you have one) |
| ☐ Tech-support number of ISP | ☐ List of country codes (included in this book) |

# Popular U.S. Mobile Phone Carriers

| CARRIER | NETWORK | INTERNATIONAL? | CONTACT |
|---------|---------|----------------|---------|
| AT&T Wireless | TDMA GSM/GPRS  3G: EDGE | Yes* | www.attwireless.com<br>1-866-293-4634 |
| Cingular Wireless | TDMA GSM/GPRS  3G: EDGE | Yes* | www.cingular.com<br>1-800-331-0500 |
| Sprint PCS | CDMA | No** | www.sprintpcs.com<br>1-888-211-4727 |
| T-Mobile | GSM/GPRS | Yes | www.t-mobile.com<br>1-800-T-MOBILE |
| Nextel | IDEN | No** | www.nextel.com<br>1-800-639-6111 |
| Verizon Wireless | CDMA | No** | www.verizonwireless.com<br>1-800-922-0204 |
| Metro PCS | CDMA | No** | www.metropcs.com<br>1-888-863-8768 |

*As of press time, AT&T and Cingular Wireless are merging, and Sprint and Nextel are merging.

**If you have a CDMA phone, it might work outside the USA in regions such as Canada, Puerto Rico, and the U.S. Virgin Islands. Check with your carrier for more information on traveling with your phone.

# Some Standard Plug Adapters

| | |
|---|---|
| | This three-prong plug is typically used in England, Hong Kong, Ireland, Jordan, Kuwait, Malaysia, Saudi Arabia, Singapore, Wales, Zambia, and more. |
| | This two-prong, rounded plug is typically used throughout Western Europe, Scandinavia, and many parts of Eastern Europe, as well as Egypt, Iran, Israel, the Philippines, Thailand, Turkey, and more. |
| | This two-prong plug is typically used in the USA, Bermuda, Canada, most of Central America, Cuba, Haiti, Jamaica, Japan, Mexico, Puerto Rico, Venezuela, the Virgin Islands, and more. |
| | This two-prong plug with flat, angled prongs (shaped like a "V") is commonly used in Australia, China, Fiji, New Zealand, Western Samoa, and more. |

## More travel resources

To see a complete list of plug adapters, voltage considerations, and travel information, bookmark these Web sites. Some of them sell travel gear, including phone jacks for foreign countries!

- Steve Kropla's Help for World Travelers (www.kropla.com)

- Voltage Valet (www.voltagevalet.com)

- Laptop Travel (www.laptoptravel.com)

- Escape Artist (www.escapeartist.com)

- Voltage Converter Transformers (www.voltage-converter-transformers.com)

# Voltages Around the World

| | |
|---|---|
| **110/120v** | American Samoa, Antilles (St. Martin), Bahamas, Barbados, Belize, Bermuda, Brazil, Canada, Cayman Islands, Colombia, Costa Rica, Dominican Republic, El Salvador, Guam, Guatemala, Haiti, Honduras, Jamaica, Liberia, Micronesia, Nicaragua, Palau, Panama, Philippines, Puerto Rico, Saba/Statia, Taiwan, Tobago, Trinidad, USA, Venezuela, Virgin Islands. |
| **220/240v** | Albania, Afghanistan, Angola, Anguilla, Antigua/Barbuda, Argentina, Armenia, Australia, Austria, Azerbaijan, Azores, Bahrain, Balearic Islands, Bali, Belarus, Belgium, Benin, Bhutan, Bosnia-Herzegovina, Botswana, Brunei, Bulgaria, Burkina Faso, Burma (Myanmar), Burundi, Byelorussia, Cameroon, Cape Verde Islands, Central African Republic, Chad, Channel Islands, Chile, China, Comoros, Congo, Cote d'Ivoire, Croatia, Cyprus, Czech Republic, Denmark, Djibouti, Dominica, Egypt, England, Eritrea, Estonia, Ethiopia, Faeroe Islands, Fiji, Finland, France, French Guiana, Gabon, Gambia, Georgia, Germany, Ghana, Gibraltar, Greece, Greenland, Grenada, Grenadines, Guadeloupe, Guinea, Hong Kong, Hungary, Iceland, India, Iran, Iraq, Ireland, Isle of Man, Israel, Italy, Ivory Coast, Jordan, Kazakhstan, Kenya, Kiribati, Kuwait, Kyrgyzstan, Latvia, Laos, Lesotho, Liechtenstein, Lithuania, Luxembourg, Macau, Macedonia, Madeira, Malawi, Malaysia, Maldives, Mali, Malta, Mauritania, Mauritius, Moldavia, Monaco, Mongolia, Montserrat, Montenegro, Mozambique, Namibia, Nauru, Nepal, Netherlands, New Caledonia, New Zealand, Niger, Nigeria, Northern Ireland, Norway, Oman, Pakistan, Papua New Guinea, Paraguay, Poland, Portugal, Romania, Russia, Rwanda, St. Kitts-Nevis, St. Lucia, St. Vincent, Senegal, Serbia, Seychelles, Sierra Leone, Singapore, Slovenia, Soloman Islands, South Africa, Spain, Sri Lanka, Sudan, Swaziland, Sweden, Switzerland, Syria, Tadzhikstan, Thailand, Tonga, Turkey, Turkmenistan, Uganda, Ukraine, United Arab Emirates, Uruguay, Uzbekistan, Wales, Western Samoa, Yemen, Yugoslavia, Zaire, Zambia, Zimbabwe |
| **Other** | Algeria (127/220), Antilles/Neth (127/220), Aruba (127/220), Bolivia (110/230), Cambodia (120/220), Canary Islands (127), Cuba (120/220), Curacao (110/220), Ecuador (120/127), Guyana (120/240), Guinea/Equatorial (150/220), Indonesia (127/220), Japan (110), Korea (110/220), Lebanon (110/220), Libya (127/220), Martinique (110/220), Mexico (127), Morocco (127/220), Okinawa (100), Peru (110/220), Saudi Arabia (127/220), Suriname (127/220), Togo (127/220), Tunisia (127/220), Vietnam (127/220). |

# CHAPTER TWO

# In Transit

*Once you're on the road, home is where your laptop is. There are several things the* Global Mobile *traveler needs to keep in mind when away from home base. You may be away from your safety net, but fortunately, the Internet is never very far away.*

# Sitting at the Gate

You've navigated through airport security, snagged a coffee, and now you're sitting comfortably at the gate awaiting the cattle-call to board the plane. What will you do?

This is an excellent time to think once more about the gear you've packed. Take a quick inventory of the plugs and adapters you'll need to stay connected at your destination. If something is missing, the airport gift shop is a great place to pick it up.

If you've got all your goodies, relax. Or get some last-minute online time while you wait for the plane—send off a few emails, check the weather at your destination, or check the latest headline news. The easiest way to do this is to connect your laptop to a Wi-Fi network. At airports where Wi-Fi is available (see page 22), the process for connecting is surprisingly easy—though often not free—and some airlines reserve this convenience for those coveted passengers who have access to the utopian airport lounge.

*You'll find signs at airport Wi-Fi hotspots that let you know where you can log on.*

### Cell yell

Have you noticed that some people (not you, of course) tend to speak about five decibels louder when they're talking on their cell phones? This phenomenon has been named *cell yell* and has given rise to a Web site devoted to cell manners (www.cellman-ners.com). If you don't know what cell yell is, you may be a perpetrator. This natural incli-nation to talk louder when on a mobile phone may come from the days of old when you could barely hear the other person, or maybe it's from the days of Dixie cup string phones. Talking louder on your phone may help the other person hear you more clearly, but it also helps everyone else within a quar-ter-mile radius of you know exactly what you're planning. So, in a word… Shhhhhh! People deserve to *not* hear your conversation.

*Some computers don't automatically switch out of Ethernet mode when you want to locate wireless networks. You might need to switch your network settings manually, and your TCP/IP settings, which allow you to connect to the Internet, should allow DHCP (automatically assigned IP addresses).*

## HOW TO GET ONLINE WITH WI-FI

1. Choose your wireless card setting in your network preferences and open your Internet connection to get online.

2. Open your Web browser and attempt to go to a Web site.

3. The Wi-Fi network will intercept your request and direct you to a "give us some money first" page (or, if you are lucky to find a free service, you might be prompted to enter a name and password, which the provider will supply).

4. After entering your credit card number and specifying how much time you want, you'll be connected to the Internet, free to browse to any site, use email, and so on.

*In this Apple PowerBook's network settings, the wireless card settings were selected from the Location pull-down menu, and the green light next to the AirPort selection indicates that the laptop is connected to the Internet via Wi-Fi.*

IN TRANSIT

## The hottest spots

Some of the most frequently traveled airports now have wireless access. More and more airports are adding this service because customers are demanding it, and it generates a significant amount of revenue for the provider. A few airports that currently offer Wi-Fi access are:

Denver International Airport

Japan's Narita International Airport

London's Heathrow International Airport

Munich International Airport

Newark Liberty International Airport

San Francisco International Airport

San Jose Minetta International Airport

Vienna International Airport

For a global listing of some Wi-Fi-friendly airports, check www.ezgoal.com/hotspots/ or, for free locations, try www.wififreespot.com/

Yes, it's just that simple. This is a great way to retrieve recent emails and keep them for responding to later. You'll have plenty of time to type on the plane, for example. But unless you're on one of those airlines that offers broadband access, you won't be able to actually send your replies until you're in an airport again or safely checked into your room.

*To save battery power, you might also want to dim the brightness on your screen and keep your laptop in sleep mode as much as possible.*

Also, if you're using your computer while sitting at the gate, try to find one of the coveted seats adjacent to a power outlet. Once you're captive in coach seating—particularly on an international flight—precious battery power becomes like water in the desert. Expired battery? No DVDs, no gaming, no nothing. Basically your computer becomes dead weight, and you'll resent the fact that you have to lug it around until you're able to recharge it. My advice is to invest in a second battery, and try to avoid using it by plugging into an outlet whenever you can.

This same battery advice applies to your mobile phone as well. Yacking on the phone while at the gate may ultimately prove to be your undoing at your destination. Not having enough battery juice to call your friends or a cab when you arrive is not cool. If you know you'll be talking a fair amount between charges, consider getting a second battery for your phone (if it supports this).

## On the Plane

If you're used to having your mobile phone ready and willing to answer the call of duty at all times, you may feel a bit naked when the flight attendant tells you to shut your phone off for the remainder of the flight.

As long as you've got your trusty laptop (and, hopefully, have charged its battery), you'll have plenty to keep your mind distracted during the flight. And if you're lucky enough to be on a flight that actually has broadband Internet access, you can communicate in any number of ways—instant messaging with friends across the globe, video chatting, voice over IP (which allows phone calls over the Internet—see Chapter 8), and so forth.

### Flyin' with Wi-Fi

Remember when it was a novelty just to make an overpriced phone call from your seat? Well, if the FCC and the airline carriers have their way, you'll be able to connect wirelessly to the Internet at broadband speeds.

As of this writing, the airlines already experimenting with the broadband wagon are Korean Airlines, Lufthansa, Scandinavian Airlines System, Japan Airlines, ANA, Singapore Airlines, and China Airlines. So far, no U.S. carriers have announced this capability—however, Qualcomm and American Airlines have tested in-cabin mobile phone usage using CDMA mobile phones on an American Airlines aircraft. Through an in-cabin cellular network, passengers on the test flight were able to place and receive calls, send and receive text messages, and check voicemail as if they were on the ground.

 *It's not just the airlines that are providing Wi-Fi for their customers. A Boston bus company called LimoLiner (www.limoliner.com) provides wireless Internet access on trips between Boston and New York City—plus power outlets for your laptop, DVDs of the latest movies, and more.*

## On Arrival

When you arrive at your destination, and the flight attendant says it's safe to reactivate all electronic devices, you'll finally be able to turn your phone on again. If you are traveling domestically, you'll want to make sure your phone can find your home network or at least a network with which your carrier has a roaming agreement. If you're traveling internationally, you'll want to make sure you're able to connect to the network and make phone calls. You might have to switch frequency bands on your cell phone when you arrive—for example, switching from 1900 GSM in North America to 900/1800 GSM in Europe, Asia, or Africa.

# CHAPTER THREE

# At Your Destination

*Home, sweet temporary home. Whether you're staying at a hotel or with friends or family, the first thing you'll probably want to do is throw yourself onto the bed and breathe "ahhhh" in sheer relief. Next you might plug in and charge your laptop and cell phone so that they can have that same "ahhhh, home" feeling. And finally, if you haven't had the chance to check your email while on the road, you probably want to connect to the Internet using the nearest available connection, be it wireless or wired.*

*If you're staying at a hotel and you weren't able to find one that offers wireless access (see Chapter 1), you can create your own Wi-Fi hotspot right in your room to increase your mobility. If not, you'll probably have to suffer through being attached at the hip (or Ethernet port) to the desk in your room—or worse (shudder), using your laptop's built-in dial-up modem with a phone cable.*

# Connecting via Ethernet Broadband

If you packed correctly, you already have the correct Ethernet cable (a straight-through category 5 with RJ-45 connectors at either end) with you and can plug it into the Ethernet port in your room. (If you don't have your trusty cable, you may be able to get one from the hotel concierge or front desk.) Basically, an Ethernet cable looks like a super-sized telephone cable.

*When buying an Ethernet cable, be sure to specify a "straight-through" cable as opposed to a "crossover" cable. It's impossible to tell the difference just by looking at them, but crossover cables have a flipped pair of wires inside and don't work with most computers.*

Now that you've juiced up your computer and plugged into the Ethernet (and have finished rolling around or jumping on the bed), it's time to connect and pay the hotel fee to open the data pipe to your room. Nothing could be simpler at this point: Just launch your favorite Web browser and try to go to any Web page. The hotel's server will intercept your page request and re-route you to its "gimme some money" e-commerce system. You'll be presented with a screen that outlines different levels of service and the fees for each. Pick one, enter your credit card number, and you're off. This is the basic routine that millions of travelers perform daily.

So, what makes you different from the other notebook-toting, cell phone-slinging lemmings? You've got this book, for one thing. Let's take a step beyond just plugging in and logging on and see how else you can wield your *Global Mobile* power.

# Connecting via Wi-Fi

Connecting to a hotel's wireless network is very similar to connecting to the one at your local Starbucks, except you have the option to add the connection charges to your room's bill.

*Some hotels haven't made the leap to offering wireless Internet access in all of their rooms. Instead, the usual "toe-in-the-water" step is to offer access in the main common areas such as the lobby. For example, on a recent business trip to New York I stayed at the W Tuscany Hotel in Manhattan, which offered Ethernet access in the rooms and Wi-Fi in the common areas.*

Make sure your computer's preferences are set to use wireless networking. The wireless connection procedure is nearly identical to connecting with the Ethernet port (see preceding section). Launch your browser and attempt to access any Web page. As with Ethernet, the hotel's server will intercept your request and present you with a payment options page.

## Do-It-Yourself Hotel Wi-Fi

Even though many hotels do not yet offer wireless access in their rooms, there's no reason why you can't take matters into your own hands and make your room wireless. Several products are on the market that let you plug a Wi-Fi base station into an Ethernet jack—such as the one in your room. Bringing your own portable wireless base station lets you move freely about your room and do your work from wherever. It's perfect for those who like to multitask in the bathroom.

Typically, a portable wireless base station plugs into a wall outlet for power and has an Ethernet port into which you connect the cable from the hotel's Ethernet jack. It then communicates wirelessly with the Wi-Fi card in your laptop, giving you a magical invisible cable that releases you from the confines of your room's Internet port.

*Because you're essentially creating your own hotspot in the hotel, you can also share your Internet access with your traveling companions—which means they can help defer the cost.*

A number of products on the market are designed to help you go wireless on the road. Check out the Pocket Router/AP from D-Link (www.dlink.com), or Apple's AirPort Express (www.apple.com/airportexpress). These products are a snap to set up and usually come with clear, concise instructions to get you up and surfing quickly. For the frequent road warrior, I recommend keeping one of these devices in your luggage and making the establishment of a wireless access point a standard part of your "prep the room" regimen.

## Locking down your network

Be sure to require a password for access to your own private hot-spot—you don't want everyone in the hotel getting a free ride, soaking up your bandwidth, poking around your personal files, installing malicious software, or worse. You can control access using the configuration software that comes with your base station.

Considering that the very nature of wireless access means that anyone within range of an access point can see that network, it makes sense to take further precautions. Depending on the documentation that came with your particular base station, you will have the option to do any or all of the following:

- **Turn off SSID** (Set Service Identifier) so that your base station and network will only appear to those that enter its name.

- **Enable password protection** so that everyone can see the name of your network, but only those who have the password can access it.

- **Use WEP (Wired Equivalent Privacy)**, a level of security that allows you, the administrator, to define a set of "keys" for each person that wants to access the network. Keys pass through an encryption algorithm before access is granted.

- **Set up pre-approved MAC (Media Access Control) addresses.** Every network card (Ethernet or wireless) has a unique address assigned to it. This address acts like a thumbprint for that particular computer. As network administrator, you can restrict access to only those MAC addresses that you deem worthy. Once those machines are added to the list, they'll never have to use a password, because their MAC addresses serve as their authentication.

## How much does portable wireless cost?

In the Wi-Fi world, there are currently two dominant flavors to choose from. 802.11b, at 11 Mbps, is the older and more established Wi-Fi standard, but the newer, stronger, faster kid on the block is 802.11g, which screams along at up to 54 Mbps.

- D-Link's AirPlus G DWL-G730AP Wireless Pocket Router/AP ($99) is a portable device that creates an 802.11g (Wi-Fi) wireless network. (www.dlink.com/products/?pid=346)

- Netgear's WGR101 Wireless Travel Router ($75-100) provides 802.11g wireless connectivity. (http://netgear.com/products/details/WGR101.php)

- Apple Computer's Airport Express ($100) provides both 802.11g and 802.11b access. (www.apple.com/airportexpress)

For more prices, check out Froogle, Google's price comparison tool (www.froogle.com). Search for *portable base station*.

## Advantages of portable wireless over Ethernet

Sometimes Wi-Fi is not just more convenient than wired access—it's actually better. Here are a few circumstances where wireless access prevails over wired—keep these scenarios in mind the next time you're on a business trip:

- You and your traveling companions would like to hold meetings in a hotel conference room or suite, but the room only offers one wired Internet connection jack. If you're using a portable wireless access point, you can share that single connection.

■ You're sharing a hotel room with your significant other or a colleague. Both of you desperately need to check email and your company's stock price. With a portable hotspot, you don't have to take turns, provided you each have wireless-enabled laptops.

■ The hotel room's Internet connection is located on its rather ill-conceived, ergonomically challenged desk, and you'd rather hop on the Internet and check email from the bed or another area in the room.

Each of these scenarios presents a plausible reason for adding a portable hotspot to your bag of tricks. You don't *have* to be wireless in your room, but it does make things easier. Apple's AirPort Express is small enough to slip into your bag and easy enough to set up that it makes a welcome addition to any wireless road warrior's arsenal.

## Connecting via Dial-up Modem

When all else fails, you might need to dial up to the Internet the old-fashioned way: by connecting your built-in modem to a phone cable that's plugged into a phone jack or the data port on the side of your room telephone.

You should bring your Internet Service Provider's (ISP) local, toll-free, or Internet dial-up numbers that you'll need to use while you're on the road. Be aware that most ISPs will charge an additional roaming fee to use these numbers. And, if you're staying at a hotel, you'll probably be charged additional dialing fees even for local calls.

Though you should have created and tested your network settings options before you left home, the following section shows how to set up your laptop's internal modem to connect to the Internet—make sure that you *have* a modem! Take a quick peek at the back

*To get a list of local dial-up phone numbers for your ISP before you go on the road, either visit its Web site or try looking on the List of ISPs (www.thelist.com) to see if the area you're visiting is serviced by your current plan.*

## What's a DNS number?

DNS (Domain Name Service) numbers are the numerical IP addresses associated with an Internet domain. Usually you know your domain by an alphabetic name, but behind all these clever names is an unmemorable address made up of numbers. Some ISPs will serve your DNS numbers to you automatically, and others require you to enter these numbers into your network settings manually before you can get online. Just to make sure you stay connected, get your DNS numbers from your ISP before you leave.

of your laptop—if you see a jack with a phone icon next to it, you probably have a modem. If you don't have one installed, you can pick up either a USB-based or a PC Card modem from almost any computer hardware retailer.

### To configure Windows XP dial-up access

1. Gather this information from your Internet Service Provider (ISP):

   ■ Username and password

   ■ Dial-up access phone number

   ■ DNS numbers for your ISP

2. From the Start menu, choose Control Panel.

3. Double-click the Network Connections icon.

*If your screen is in Category view, it might be easier to configure if you switch it back to Classic view.*

4.   Click Create a new connection under Network Tasks.

5.   On the New Connection Wizard Welcome screen that appears, click the Next button. When the Network Connection Type screen appears, select Connect to the Internet and click the Next button.

6.   Select Set up my connection manually and click the Next button.

7.   Select Connect using a dial-up modem and click the Next button.

8.   In the ISP Name field, type a name to identify your connection (for example, *On the Road Jack*) and click the Next button.

9.   In the Phone number field, type your ISP's dial-up access phone number (from step 1) and click the Next button.

10.   In the User name field, type your email address.

11.   In the Password field, type your password.

12.   In the Confirm password field, retype your password.

13.   Uncheck the box next to "Use this account name and password when anyone connects to the Internet from this computer."

14.   Uncheck the box next to "Make this the default Internet connection."

15.   Check the box next to "Add a shortcut to this connection to my Desktop" (only if you want this) and click the Finish button.

16.   Consider staying someplace that has high-speed Internet access next time.

*If you're staying at a hotel, be sure to add the prefix (often a "9") to your phone number so that you can access an outside telephone line.*

## To configure Mac OS X dial-up access

1.  Gather this information from your Internet Service Provider (ISP):

    ■ Username and password

    ■ Dial-up access phone number

    ■ DNS numbers for your ISP

2.  Choose Apple > System Preferences.

3.  Choose View > Network.

4.  Choose Show > Internal Modem.

5.  Click the PPP button.

6.  Type the information you gathered in step 1 into the corresponding fields.

Your username goes in the Account Name field. If you want the other users of this computer to use the same connection method, select the checkbox for "Save password." In the Telephone Number field, don't forget to prefix the ISP's dial-up number with any numbers that your hotel requires to get an outside line, and it can't hurt to place a comma before the access number so that the modem pauses briefly during dialing.

7.   Click the TCP/IP tab.

Choose either *PPP* or *Manually* from the Configure pop-up menu, as instructed by your Internet Service Provider.

Choosing PPP allows your provider to automatically assign you an IP address when you connect. Choosing Manually is appropriate if your ISP gave you a static IP address. This static IP address would be entered in the IP address field.

8.   Enter the DNS addresses in the corresponding field, if your ISP requires you to manually enter them.

With some ISPs, DNS addresses are dynamically supplied to you (meaning you don't need to know them).

9.   Click Apply Now.

10.  Click Connect Now and wait for the old-fashioned modem sounds. When the Authentication and Connect process is complete, open a Web browser to verify your connection to the Internet.

11.  Consider staying at a hotel that has high-speed Internet access next time.

# Dialing Internationally

No matter where you're staying while you're on the road, you can't just rely on the Internet—you might need to make international phone calls, too. Depending on what country you're in when you make the call, and what country you're trying to reach, you might not be able to remember the numbers you need to dial to make sure you get Paris, France, and not Paris, Texas.

Appendix B includes a full list of country codes and international access numbers to help you with that often-perplexing problem. But first, let's take a look at the different ways to get your call out of the country.

If you're staying at a hotel, take a look at the instructions near your hotel's phone and see if they list an access number for a long-distance line from your room. Some hotels require that you simply press 9 for any outside line; others have a different digit for long-distance or international; and still others require you to call the front desk and have the person there place the call for you.

### INTERNATIONAL DIRECT-DIAL ACCESS CODES

You'll need to use an international direct-dial access code to get an international phone line. These numbers vary, but are not unique to each country—for example, the United States and Canada both use 011 to get an international line, and most parts of Europe use 00. (See Appendix B for more on international direct-dial numbers.)

### COUNTRY CODES

The country code is the national prefix that you must use when dialing a number in that particular country from another country. In most cases you will also need to dial a city or area code as well. For example, the city prefixes in most of Europe are anywhere from one to four digits (such as 1 for Paris, 20 for Amsterdam, and 6221 for Heidelberg), whereas the U.S. uses a three-digit area code, such as 212 for parts of New York City.

## International phone dialing 101

The numbers that you dial when you make an international phone call vary, depending on the location you're calling and from where you're calling. For example, suppose you're in the United States and you're trying to dial a buddy in Paris. You would dial the following:

011 [USA international access code] +

33 [the country code for France] +

1 [the city code for Paris] +

23 45 67 [the phone number]

Now, to make things more confusing, you might have looked on the Internet for the number that you want to call in Paris and found it listed as 01 23 45 67, adding an additional 0 prefix in front of the Paris city code. This is the phone number that you would dial if you were *already* in France, or were calling from within Paris.

Many cities in Europe add a 0 at the beginning of their phone numbers, which is used for dialing within their own country. This 0 gets dropped when telephoning that number from outside that particular country.

If you were dialing this same friend at the same Parisian telephone number from another European country, you would dial the following:

00 [European international access code] +

33 [the country code for France] +

1 [the city code for Paris] +

23 45 67 [the phone number]

Finally, if you want to phone a friend in the U.S. from Europe, you'd also need to dial 00 first for international access, then 1 (the country code for the United States), and then the area code and phone number that you want to reach.

And remember, it's a lot cheaper to send text messages overseas from your mobile phone to another mobile—see Chapter 6.

# CHAPTER FOUR

# Working While on the Road

*Most road warriors know they don't need to go to their offices to get work done—their work-places are the tools they carry wherever they go. You, too, can discover the joys (and the disadvantages) of being able to take care of business, remotely, from almost anyplace in the world—from securely accessing corporate email to printing, faxing, and more.*

# Accessing a Virtual Private Network Remotely

If you work in an office environment and tote your laptop between home, work, and travel locations, chances are you already know about Virtual Private Networks (VPNs). If you don't, you're in for a pleasant, productivity-enhancing surprise. A VPN allows certain authorized employees of a company to access its private network when they're not at the office. Virtual Private Networks work by using the Internet or other "public" carriers as a transit system for private network traffic, usually in encrypted form. You will find it to be indispensable in your travels.

 *Intervention needed? That fantasy of working at the beach with your laptop is now a reality. However, why anyone would bring his or her computer to the beach is a topic for another book. Just say "no."*

Think of a company with multiple offices located around the globe—the employees all need access to the same files and to each other, but of course allowing the entire world to access their network goodies is out of the question. A VPN allows them to operate as if they were all in the same office building. They can transfer files, use company databases, access their email, and print documents.

## How a VPN works

A VPN is secure; the data sent across the public Internet is encrypted, so that the data transferred is private. Using the Internet, two offices can merge their networks into one network by encrypting traffic that uses the Internet link. A good way to think about VPNs is as buildings connected by elevated walkways. That walkway allows the occupants of the buildings free access to one another while keeping out the people on the ground.

A *Remote-Access VPN* is a type of VPN designed for the mobile or remote user, typically one who works for a large company with hundreds of people deployed in the field. To connect to a Remote-Access

VPN you need an account and a password. Rather than assign a simple text password that might be easily cracked or guessed, many companies give their employees small hardware devices called *fobs* that can be carried on keychains. Each fob displays a new random number at regular intervals. To log into the VPN, the employee must enter both a previously assigned PIN (Personal Identification Number) as well as the number on the fob. This dual-authentication system ensures that only authorized users can connect to the VPN. There are various types of VPN implementations, so it's best to check with your network administrator to learn the particulars of your company's set up.

*This fob issues randomly generated security numbers and changes them regularly.*

Once set up, VPNs are very easy to use and almost transparent to the user.

**CONNECTING TO A VPN**

1. Ensure you are connected to the Internet, either by dial-up, wireless, or Ethernet connection.

2. Launch the VPN software (provided by your network administrator).

3. Provide your user name and PIN (and fob number if you have one).

4. Get to work.

It's that simple. Once you are connected to the Internet, it's relatively simple to attach to a VPN network. Once connected, your computer has all the rights and privileges that you'd have if you were seated at your desk in the office. It's very liberating to be able to get work done from anyplace on the planet with Internet access, and that's a whole lotta places.

### REASONS TO CONNECT VIA VPN

Email is probably the most popular reason people connect to their networks via VPN. Many times it is not possible to retrieve your corporate email unless you are connected to the corporate network. VPN-ing into the network lets you retrieve and respond to email from your corporate email address instead of your personal email account (which reveals that you're not in the office).

Utilizing corporate intranet resources is another reason why people VPN into their corporate networks. Accessing human resource information, downloading company software, or even checking to see how many vacation days you've got left are all possible while sitting in your hotel room once you've successfully VPN-ed into your corporate network.

Another reason to VPN into a network is for server administration. I know this is a little geeky, but many network administrators are able to live relatively normal lives largely due to the freedom VPN affords them. They can VPN into the network to check the status of servers, install software on them, or otherwise control and maintain the network from wherever they happen to be. The Internet is the great liberator, and VPN unlocks it so that you can be just as productive sitting at an Internet café as you are in your mind-numbing cubicle. If you haven't done so already, contact your system administrator and have them set you up for VPN access.

# Printing and Faxing on the Road

One of the luxuries of working from an office—even your home office—is that you have access to office amenities such as office printers and fax machines. When you're on the road, you may find yourself in need of these tools. Let's look at a few ways you can have the benefits of your work or home office using some smart *Global Mobile* thinking.

## Printing via hotel fax machine

Imagine that you check into your hotel room and discover you need a hard copy of a document for a meeting that occurs in a few hours, and there are no printers available. If your laptop comes with an internal modem capable of sending and receiving faxes, consider using your computer's built-in faxing capabilities to send a fax to yourself at the hotel's front desk. The process is extremely simple—you are essentially "printing" a document to a remote fax machine.

This works in a pinch, though bear in mind that the hard copy may be less than crisp, depending on the fax machine. Also, most fax machines print header and footer information on every page, breaking the illusion of a document produced on a normal printer. Additionally, some hotels still use thermal (curly and thin) paper. Finally, consider that hotels may charge a pretty penny for each page you fax to yourself (only you can determine whether using this method is acceptable and worthwhile). But, in a pinch, self-faxing works.

*If you don't have a modem already installed, now is the time to get one. You can pick up a decent modem for under $30 from any computer retailer.*

Take some time to learn the faxing software that came with your computer. Both Windows XP and Mac OS X (10.3 and above) ship with faxing capabilities, but you need to configure them first. Of course, even with properly configured software, you need to have a fax-capable modem in your computer, and it must be connected to an analog phone line with a normal telephone cord with RJ-11 jacks on both ends.

## Bluetooth printing

Bluetooth printers are becoming more commonplace. Bluetooth, as discussed in Chapter 7, is a short-range wireless networking technology. It's primarily used to connect devices and peripherals to each other and your computer without cumbersome cables. If you come across a Bluetooth-enabled printer when you're on the road, and you have a Bluetooth-enabled laptop, you can send your documents wirelessly to it at a nearby office or even a copy store.

Anyone who has access to a Bluetooth printer can print to it within 30 feet or so. Laptops and PDAs alike can do this. Many printer manufacturers (including Hewlett-Packard and Epson) offer Bluetooth-enabled printers—check the Web sites of these companies for information on the latest models that offer Bluetooth connectivity and hope that you encounter one on your travels.

**SETTING UP AND CONFIGURING WINDOWS XP FAX**

Although faxing capabilities come with Windows XP, they aren't turned on by default. However, by running the Fax Configuration Wizard, you can set up your PC to both send and receive faxes.

1. Choose Start > Control Panel and click Add or Remove Programs.

2. Click Add/Remove Windows Components. Select only the "Fax Services" checkbox and click Next.

3. Choose Start > All Programs > Accessories > Communications > Fax > Fax Console (the center of XP's faxing universe).

4.  In the Fax Console application, choose Tools > Configure Fax. This opens the Fax Configuration Wizard. Click Next.

5.  On the Sender Information page, include your name or your business name and your fax number and anything else you'd like your recipients to know.

6.  On the Select Device for Sending or Receiving Faxes screen, your modem will already be selected unless you have more than one. (In that case, select the right one.) Specify send and receive options and whether you'd like to manually or automatically answer incoming faxes.

    Choosing "manual" will require you to click File > Receive a fax every time you answer the phone and hear a fax noise. Choosing "automatic" enables your laptop to manage the incoming call.

7.  On the Transmitting Subscriber Identification (TSID) and Called Subscriber Identification (CSID) screens, input your business name and fax number.

8.  On the Routing Options screen, specify how incoming faxes will be handled. All of your faxes are stored automatically in the Fax Console, but you can also print a copy.

If you want to change any of these settings, just run the Fax Configuration Wizard again. To open the wizard, choose Tools > Configure Fax.

Now that you're set up, you can fax pretty much any document on your computer. Simply choose Fax Printer as the output device when you print. This will initiate the Fax Console, where you'll choose the recipient and enter the fax number.

**SETTING UP AND CONFIGURING MAC OS X FAX**

The following instructions only apply to Mac OS X 10.3 (Panther) and above. (To add faxing capabilities to earlier versions of the Macintosh operating system, consider buying a third-party application page-sender—see www.smileonmymac.com.)

1. Open the document you want to fax.

2. Choose File > Print.

3. Click Fax (at the bottom of the Print dialog box).

4. Type the fax number of the user to whom you want to send your fax in the To field.

5. If necessary, type the dialing prefix required for the phone system you're using in the Dialing Prefix field. (For example, if you need to dial a 9 to access an outside line, type 9 in the Dialing Prefix field.)

6. Make sure the desired modem is chosen in the Modem pop-up menu.

7. If you want to send a cover page, select the Cover Page checkbox and type a message in the large field below.

8. Click Fax. The fax will be sent as soon as your modem is available.

   If you're using your modem to access your dial-up account, the fax will be sent after you disconnect from the 'net. Unless you sign up for a virtual, Internet-based faxing service (such as www.efax.com), your fax will be sent using old analog telephone technology and not transmitted digitally over the Internet.

*You can also pick users directly from the Address Book by clicking its icon to the right of the To field. Just make sure you have a fax number listed for each user you choose.*

*If you have a combination of options that you frequently use when faxing a document, you can save them as a "preset." After choosing your options, choose Save As from the Presets pop-up menu and type a name for the set of options. If you want to use this set of options when you fax a document, choose its name from the Presets pop-up menu.*

**RECEIVING FAXES ON YOUR MAC**

In addition to sending faxes using your Mac's modem, you can also receive them, provided your computer has been set up properly in advance. The incoming fax is saved as a graphics file on your hard drive, allowing you to view, print, and forward it using the same programs you already use for your other graphics files. You can even select how you want to be notified that you've received a fax. For example, you can have incoming faxes print automatically or be forwarded to you via email.

1.  Choose Apple > System Preferences and then click Print & Fax.

2.  Click Faxing to display the fax options.

3.  Select the "Receive faxes on this computer" checkbox.

4.  Enter your fax number in the field provided. This will show up on the sending fax machine's display or status report.

5.  Enter the number of times you want your phone line to ring before your machine receives the call as a fax.

    If you have a phone-answering machine or message center, you should set this number at a higher number of rings than your message service, otherwise all incoming calls will be intercepted by your laptop.

6.  Choose one or more of the options you'd like performed after a fax arrives:

    ▪ Save it as a graphics file to a particular folder or the desktop

    ▪ Automatically email it as an attachment to a particular email address

    ▪ Print it on a designated printer

ON THE ROAD

That's it. The next time your phone rings, the computer will answer after the specified number of rings and act just like a normal fax machine. This can be annoying for human callers if you don't have your modem connected to a dedicated fax line, so try to pick up the phone before your computer does, unless you're expecting a fax transmission.

Remember: To receive a fax, your computer must be turned on and connected to an open telephone line. If you're using your modem to connect to the Internet, it can't receive a fax at the same time.

 *If your Energy Saver preferences automatically put your Mac to sleep after a certain period of inactivity, select the "Wake when the modem detects a ring" checkbox in the Options pane to avoid missing any incoming faxes.*

## Backing up Your Files

One of the worst things that can happen to the *Global Mobile* traveler is to lose one or more pieces of gear. Computers, PDAs, cell phones, iPods, and other gear are not cheap. And if your data is more valuable than the device itself, you begin to realize how crazy it is to travel without an adequate backup of at least your most critical files. Following are a few ways to hedge your bets against catastrophic equipment loss—whether by theft or simple hardware or software failure.

The time to think about safeguarding your files is *before* you hit the road. "Woulda-shoulda-coulda" won't help you salvage that presentation you worked on all night. Making a copy of your critical data will not only give you peace of mind, but will also ensure that the show goes on. Unfortunately, most people don't realize how critical backing up their data is until *after* a system failure.

Before you leave your home on a business trip, back up your entire computer. This is easier said than done, but backing up will save you time, prevent headaches, and defend against other issues in the long run. Although it is beyond the scope of this book to detail all of your backup options, I will point out a few options you should already have available to you.

## Backing up Windows XP

Stashed away on your original Windows XP discs are a bunch of utility programs that can assist you in diagnosing problems with your system. The Backup Utility is one of them, and you should become familiar with it. It is your friend, and in the case of a catastrophic equipment failure, it will be your very *best* friend. The Windows XP Backup Utility isn't already installed on your new computer, and you can't install it using Add/Remove Windows Components either. You have to install it manually by inserting the Windows XP disc in the drive and browsing to the following location:

D:\VALUEADD\MSFT\NTBACK UP (where D is the letter of your CD drive)

Double-click on the file NTBACKUP.MSI to begin the installation.

There are several backup options within the application; check the documentation that shipped with your copy of Windows XP for instructions and tutorials on how to back up your data.

## Backup devices and options

Consider using one or more of the following ways to store your most critical data. Utilizing these relatively cheap storage options can safeguard that important and potentially irreplaceable document.

### PORTABLE HARD DRIVES

I recommend you purchase an external USB 2.0 or FireWire hard drive. With hard drive prices at an all-time low, using portable hard drives for backing up and carrying your critical data between systems has never been easier or more cost effective. Use this option when you need fast transfer speed and high capacities.

*Put yourself on a maintainable backup schedule—for instance, I personally back up my entire portable every weekend. So in a catastrophe, at most I will have lost six days of work. Always leave this backup drive safely at home. Some people (writers and photographers, for example) even go so far as to make multiple backup copies of their files, and store them in multiple locations. This ensures multiple levels of redundancy, but also adds lots of time to the backup routine. The key here is to put yourself on a routine that you'll likely stick to, not one that you'll avoid because it takes too much time to execute.*

### USB KEY DRIVES

Smaller than your thumb, portable USB key drives are currently available in capacities up to 1 GB. These little drives have all but replaced the venerable floppy disk as the method of choice for transferring small (and not so small) files quickly and easily.

### CD AND DVD

Don't forget the CD or DVD option when making your decision about which media to use. Recordable CDs or DVDs have become an amazingly cheap option. For smaller files, such as Microsoft Office documents or PDF files, consider using an inexpensive (sometimes as low as 10¢ each when bought in bulk) recordable CD, which can hold up to 700 MB of data. For larger or more numerous files, use multiple CDs or move up to DVDs, which are more expensive (usually about $1 per disc) but can hold up to 4.7 GB of uncompressed data.

### iPOD

With more and more people owning iPods, consider using yours to store data in addition to music. At the heart of every iPod is a high-capacity hard drive. Of course the iPod was designed to store and play back music, but you can also store data on the space that's not occupied by your tunes. Turn on the option to use your iPod as a disk drive from within the iPod preferences screen in iTunes.

### ONLINE DATA STORAGE

Another alternative is to consider periodically uploading your most critical files to an online data storage account, or emailing files as attachments to yourself. That way you'll always have a backup copy you can retrieve from the remote server.

CHAPTER FIVE

# In Public Places

*Even when we're not always at work or in transit, we still want to connect with others. Fortunately, technology has evolved to the point where online access—when and where you need it—is usually never far away.*

# The Hotspot Invasion

If you haven't been watching closely, you might not have noticed that Wi-Fi *hotspots* (public areas with Wi-Fi connections) are sprouting up everywhere. Businesses have recognized the demand for wireless access where people congregate, and many laptops now have built-in Wi-Fi. Wireless networks are becoming almost as prevalent as ATMs.

A few years ago, Wi-Fi was typically found in larger corporations, and even then only in those that were on the cutting edge. But then something changed. Computer manufacturers such as Dell and Apple decided that they'd make 802.11 wireless networking capabilities either an option or standard on every machine they sold. This move, coupled with Microsoft's building Wi-Fi support into Windows, jump-started the "wireless movement." Promotions for Wi-Fi access started popping up in TV commercials, in the airport, at hotels, and even in local coffee shops.

And then Starbucks percolated the idea of teaming up with T-Mobile, an Internet Service Provider, to bring wireless access (and vanilla lattes) to its thousands of stores and millions of customers. Realizing the moneymaking potential of hotspots, other fast-food establishments soon climbed onto the "lure them in with access" bandwagon. Most notable was McDonald's, which announced in 2003 that it would add Wi-Fi to its menu.

# Finding a Hotspot

When you're away from your home or business network and want to find a wireless hotspot, the best way is to do your research *before* you leave home, because the easiest way to find hotspots is to use the Web. Many Web sites list Wi-Fi-friendly coffee shops, airports, hotels, universities, libraries, and other public places.

### Getting the gear

Before you can surf, you've got to have a surfboard—in this case, a Wi-Fi card for your laptop. As I mentioned in Chapter 1, most new PCs come pre-configured with Intel's Centrino wireless technology. And most new iBooks and PowerBooks from Apple Computer come pre-configured with an AirPort card for Wi-Fi access.

But what if you don't have one of these Wi-Fi-ready machines? You're not out of luck. You can pick up a Wi-Fi card adapter at your local computer store, online reseller, or other electronics retailer for under $100. There are a few flavors of Wi-Fi currently on the market: 802.11a, 802.11b, and 802.11g. The "b" is the slowest of them all, and the most prevalent, but that doesn't mean it's too slow. 802.11b is still plenty fast for all but the most demanding of data transfers. That said, my recommendation is to pick up the fastest 802.11 card you can get your hands on (currently 802.11a or 802.11g). You may pay a bit more, but you'll be staving off technological obsolescence for a while longer. In the meantime, the newer, faster cards are also compatible with the (currently more widespread) 802.11b networks.

At Yahoo! Mobile (http://mobile.yahoo.com/wifi), you enter a street address to get a list of hotspots within a certain radius. Google works similarly: Search on the name of your town plus "Wi-Fi provider" for some probable links to information on hotspots in your community, often including mom-and-pop coffee shops and bookstores.

The following Web sites are dedicated to listing hotspots around the world:

- **HotSpotList:** www.hotspotlist.com

- **WiFi411:** www.wifi411.com

- **WiFinder:** www.wifinder.com

- **Wififreespot:** www.wififreespot.com (lists only free Wi-Fi providers)

If you're a creature of habit and pretty much know that you'll always be surfing relatively close to your home base, then you might consider signing up with T-Mobile. In the United States, T-Mobile has Wi-Fi hotspots in Borders bookstores as well as Starbucks, and they've recently announced plans to offer wireless access at 1000 Kinko's locations nationwide.

## Getting Connected

Once you've found a hotspot, you need to make sure that both your computer and the hotspot can recognize each other. This will happen automatically, as long as your wireless hardware is activated, whenever your laptop comes within range of the hotspot.

Most Windows laptops display a signal icon in the system tray, on the bottom right-hand corner of your screen, or an indicator light on the laptop itself, when the laptop finds and connects to a wireless connection. On a Macintosh, you'll see an AirPort signal-strength icon near the upper right-hand corner of your screen (provided you have selected the "Show AirPort status in menu bar" checkbox in Network preferences).

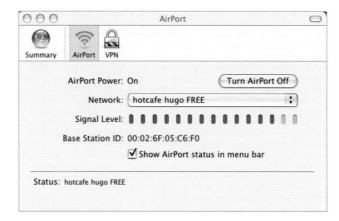

*Choosing "Open Internet Connect" from the AirPort menu signal-strength icon will show you the base stations in the area and the connection status.*

Your next step is usually to sign up with whoever is hosting or providing the hotspot and, in some cases, reconfigure your notebook according to their instructions. This is usually a matter of simply launching your Web browser, which will automatically go to the hotspot's "give me some money" page, where you may have to enter credit card information. If it's a free hotspot, you may only have to view the host's page briefly before you can go on through to the Internet.

If the hotspot you want to connect to requires payment, remember that signing up with one wireless ISP does not necessarily mean that you'll be able to connect from other branches of the same retail chain. Be sure to read the terms of service carefully before subscribing.

If you decide not to purchase a subscription, and opt for a daily or hourly usage, you'll need to use your credit card to pay for access every time you want to connect. These "pay-as-you-go" plans are better for sporadic users, and monthly plans are for those who are sure they'll get their money's worth by going the subscription route.

*T-Mobile's Wi-Fi plan offers multiple payment options.*

You should always make sure you know the fees you're being charged, as there can be a wide range of prices. And if you opt for a longer-term subscription instead of a pay-as-you-go plan, be sure to keep your username and password handy so you can sign in to the network when you return to that location.

Once you've entered your payment information, you should be immediately taken to the sign-in screen for the wireless provider. Just follow the instructions, or enter your username and password if you are already a subscriber.

*When deciding which service plan you're going to opt for, take a moment to think about how you'll use it. Will you be connecting occasionally when you need to escape from your house? Or will you be on more of a routine, connecting every morning at the same coffee shop, around the same time?*

*This café in France offers free Wi-Fi access to its customers. Passwords are provided on request by the café's staff, but you still have to go through an authentication process.*

Congratulations! You should be successfully logged on and ready to get to work. All of the usual suspects will be available to you: email, the Web, instant messaging, and so forth. At this point you can VPN into your corporate network (see Chapter 4) and really get some work done.

When you've finished surfing, remember to log off to ensure you are charged only for the time you actually used. Refer to your service provider's instructions about how to log off.

# Creating Your Own Computer-to-Computer Network

There are times when you just want to transfer a file to the person sitting right next to you. Aside from emailing it or burning it to a CD-ROM, just how *would* you transfer a 5 MB Microsoft Word document (larger than a floppy disk) to the person sitting next to you?

If both machines have Wi-Fi capability, then creating your own small, ad hoc "wireless network" to transfer files between the two machines isn't that complicated.

**TO CREATE AN AD HOC NETWORK IN WINDOWS XP**

1. Choose Start > Control Panel.

2. Double-click Network Connections to see the available network connections.

   You should see an icon representing your wireless card.

3. Right-click your wireless card's icon and choose Properties from the menu that appears.

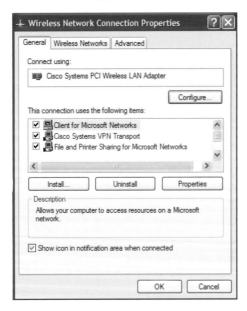

*Make sure the "Show icon in notification area when connected" checkbox is selected so that you can monitor the status of your current connection from the system tray.*

4.  Click the "Wireless Networks" tab to begin creating your wireless network.

    The screen might be empty when it first appears. To bring up the Wireless network properties window, click the Add button.

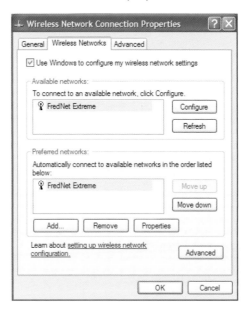

*Clicking the Add button will allow you to create, name, and add new networks.*

5.  In the Wireless Network Connection Properties window, in the Network name (SSID) field, enter the name of the network you'd like to create.

*Pick a name—any name—for your network. Just avoid using weird characters or spaces. A good rule of thumb is to stick to the letters a-z, and if you must use a space, insert an underline (_) or hyphen (-) character instead.*

You should add a password in the Network key field (and re-enter it in the Confirmation field) and give it only to those whom you want to share your ad hoc network.

6.  Select the checkbox at the bottom of the Wireless network prop-erties window labeled "This is a computer-to-computer (ad hoc) network; wireless access points are not used." Leave everything else de-selected.

7.  Click OK.

You have now properly configured your Windows XP computer to act as a host for other wireless computers—PC or Mac—in an ad hoc network.

*Until you've got everything up and running correctly, you should not select the "Data encryption (WEP enabled)" checkbox. You can do that later, after you've got every-thing humming along.*

### JOINING THE WINDOWS XP AD HOC NETWORK

If other Windows XP users want to join your network, they need to open the Network Connections control panel and double-click the wireless connection icon. Then click Properties, click the Wireless Networks tab, select the ad hoc network (that you created and named), click Configure, and then click OK.

If you go to Start > My Network Places on either computer, you should now see the *peer computer*. You now have an ad hoc network and can share files wirelessly, with nary a hotspot in sight—just drag them from one computer to the other. This technique is especially useful on flights when your traveling companion is in first class and you're stuck in coach, or if you just weren't lucky enough to score seats next to each other. You two can still continue to work, transferring files back and forth, and no one will be the wiser.

If Mac users want to join your ad hoc network, they need only choose the ad hoc network name from their AirPort menu.

### TO CREATE AN AD HOC NETWORK IN MAC OS X

Creating a peer-to-peer wireless network on the Mac is also relatively simple. Follow these steps to allow a Mac OS X-based computer to share files with other wireless computers:

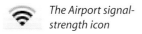
*The Airport signal-strength icon*

1.  If you don't see an AirPort signal strength indicator in the menu bar, choose Apple > System Preferences.

2.  Click the Network icon. Choose your wireless settings from the Location pop-up menu and then choose Show > Network Status. Finally, click the Configure button at the bottom of the window.

IN PUBLIC PLACES

*Click the Configure button to access your networking options.*

3.  In Network preferences, with AirPort settings shown, select the "Allow this computer to create networks" checkbox.

4.  Choose Create Network from the AirPort menu. Enter the name of the network you'd like to create.

*You can name your network anything you want, such as "PowerMac G5."*

5.  Click the Show Options button to reveal fields that allow you to set a password for accessing the network.

```
┌─────────────────────────────────────────────┐
│              Computer to Computer            │
├─────────────────────────────────────────────┤
│  Please enter the following information to   │
│  create a Computer to Computer Network:      │
│                                              │
│      Name: │ PowerMac G5                    │ │
│                                              │
│   Channel: │ Automatic (11)             ▲▼ │ │
│                                              │
│            ☐ Enable encryption (using WEP)  │
│                                              │
│  Password: │                              │ │
│                                              │
│   Confirm: │                              │ │
│                                              │
│   WEP key: │ 40–bit (more compatible)   ▲▼ │ │
│                                              │
│                                              │
│ ( Hide Options )        ( Cancel )  ( OK )  │
└─────────────────────────────────────────────┘
```

*After clicking Show Options, you can add a password for your users to ensure that your network is not available to everyone in the neighborhood.*

6.  Click OK.

    You have now properly configured your Macintosh computer to act as a host for other wireless computers—Mac or PC—in an ad hoc network.

**JOINING THE MAC OS X AD HOC NETWORK**

If other Mac users want to join your ad hoc network, they need only choose it from their AirPort menu.

If Windows XP users want to join your network, they need to open the Network Connections control panel, double-click the wireless connection icon, choose Properties, click the Wireless Networks tab, select the ad hoc network's name, click Configure, and then click OK.

CHAPTER SIX

# Text Messaging (SMS)

*While trying to decide which mobile phone to buy, a good friend of mine once asked me why would people send Short Message Service (SMS) messages—text messages—when they could just call the person instead. He had a point; I mean, after all, we as humans are lazy. Clearly, just dialing someone's number and speaking to them has got to be easier (not to mention more personal) than "triple-tapping" your way into thumb-numbness. Or is it?*

# What Is SMS?

Before I get into the startling numbers behind text messaging, let me explain what this whole "texting" business is all about. Remember back when you were in elementary school and you got caught passing notes? (Okay, maybe I'm talking about myself here.) That was text messaging: simple, to the point snippets of information. In my case, it was usually, "I like you, do you like me? Yes/No—check one." It was immediate in that I just had my best friend (the carrier) pass the note over to the cute girl in the third row. It was passive in that although I desperately wanted a response, none was required. Okay, fast forward a few decades—today, advances in wireless technology allow us to send the same sorts of passive notes (no immediate response required) to people sitting next to us in a meeting or on the other side of the planet with equal ease. Oh, by the way—that cute girl never did respond to my note.

*Text messaging is a good way to stay quietly in contact when you're on the go, which makes it perfect for* Global Mobile *travelers.*

So, why send a text message when just calling is so much more personal? Well, for several reasons. Texting can impart some critical piece of information without the whole greetings and salutations business that a traditional phone call requires. It's also good for sending information that is fairly complicated without your recipient having to write it down—an address or phone number are good examples. There are literally hundreds of uses for sending these passive notes. Perhaps you're in a situation where speaking on the phone is impossible or rude, such as sitting in a movie theater or a business meeting. Whip out your trusty mobile and text away. You won't bother a soul.

## Take a thumb break

Virgin Mobile is promoting "Safe Text" by informing its customers about how being "over-texted" can lead to RSI (Repetitive Strain Injury).

# A Brief History of Text

The very first text message was sent in December 1992—yes, over a decade ago, when T.L.C. was at the top of the pop charts. SMS was launched commercially in 1995, and by 2002 over a billion text messages were being exchanged globally per day. By 2003, that figure had jumped to almost 17 billion. One reason mobile phone carriers continue to push text messaging is that they derive up to 20% of their annual revenues* from texting. Most carriers charge 10 cents per text message sent beyond what is included in the subscriber's plan. That's a good-sized chunk of change. Also consider that 94% of 16-24 year olds—a large part of their subscriber base—use text messaging regularly.* Many of these individuals send on average 100 messages per month. According to statistics from the Mobile Data Association (MDA), U.K. mobile phone owners alone send over 55 million text messages on a typical day. In a nutshell, there's a whole lotta texting goin' on, and a whole lotta money changing hands.

And it's not showing any signs of slowing. Other services that deliver information via SMS are beginning to emerge. Yahoo!, for example, has a text-messaging service that allows its subscribers to receive stocks, weather, news, and sports information at predetermined times. For example, every day you can have your favorite five stocks pop up on your phone, or every morning at 8 a.m. have the day's forecast delivered. These types of services boggle the mind, and could never be accomplished with voice.

*According to the Media Centre at www.text.it*

## Getting your phone to read your mind

As texting becomes more popular, mobile-phone manufacturers are responding with more sophisticated handsets. Today, so-called *smart phones*, such as the palmOne Treo 600 (or 650) and the RIM Blackberry, have built-in keyboards to ease the typing hassle that other mobile-phone users experience when they have to painstakingly *triple-tap* their way to the letter they want on a standard phone keypad.

There are phones with various flavors of "predictive-typing" software, the most popular (and prevalent by far) seems to be the T9 software from Tegic Communications (www.t9.com). Tegic has nearly perfected the art of predictive typing. Predictive typing predicts what you're probably going to type; however, it's not always right. Based on the preceding word and the first few letters of the word you're working on, the phone's software will attempt to predict the current word and finish it for you. For example, if I wanted to type *I'm busy, call me later*. In actuality I might only have to type *I bu c m la*. The phone would fill in the blanks for me, depending on the level of the software's predictive-typing algorithm. This development allows for much faster and more accurate typing, and after typing a few paragraphs like this it becomes second nature as your phone seems to start reading your mind.

As of this writing, Tegic comes preinstalled on literally hundreds of mobile phone models. So, it may already be on your phone. Check the Web site to see if your phone manufacturer is listed and for some great tips on more efficient texting (www.t9.com).

*The Blackberry, left, and the Treo 650, right, are two of the most popular smart phones.*

# The Killer App?

Many people credit email for bringing the Internet widespread popularity. Yes, the World Wide Web is indispensable for finding information, buying stuff, and so on. But it was email that revolutionized the way we communicate with each other. Email killed the fax machine—or at least critically wounded it. Email killed the paper memo, the party invitation, and my penmanship skills (but at least I can type really fast now). And, of course, it brought us the dreaded *spam* message, or unsolicited junk email.

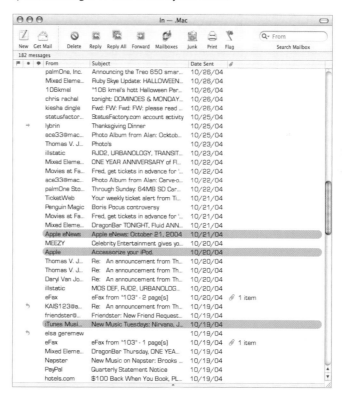

*Email was the fastest way to send someone a note until text messaging came along.*

Many experts are saying that text messaging on the phone will be the *killer app* of the mobile communications industry. And signs certainly do seem to be pointing that way. Looking at the staggering numbers already mentioned, it would seem texting has *already* become the killer app. If you think you've never received a text message, think again—the voicemail notification you receive on your mobile phone after missing a call is actually a text message. You can't escape it!

## How messages get delivered

As with email, a text message will continue trying to deliver itself to its intended recipient, but if it can't, it comes back and tells you. That is, when you send an SMS message it actually continues to "live" in the carrier's network for up to seven days; if your recipient's phone is turned off or is out of range, the message will hang out and keep trying to deliver itself for up to a week. If it still can't find the intended recipient, it will send itself back to the sender with its tail between its legs to let you know that it failed. So what all of this really means is that when you send a text message, you can be sure that it will either get to its intended recipient or come back to you. If only we could have the same level of confidence in the postal service!

The easiest way to find out if you've got texting capability is to hop on over to your carrier's Web site or, better yet, give them a call. The representative can explain what kind of text plan you currently have (if any) and if you don't have one, can set you up with one on the spot. The rep can also tell you whether your phone is capable of sending and receiving text messages or not. If you already have

---

### Phone spam

Some enterprising spammers have figured out how to send "junk text" to mobile phones. This is the ultimate in annoyance because usually recipients feel compelled to read the incoming message. And there is currently no way to filter phone spam as you can with email on your computer.

texting capability, but aren't sure how to use it, check your user's manual.

## Using the Web to send text messages

So, what are your options if you find that your current cell phone plan doesn't allow for sending or receiving text messages? Or if you're a textaholic and have run out of your allotted monthly messages, but you need to send a text message to someone's phone with some vital information—what to do? All is not lost because most, if not all, carriers maintain Web pages that allow you to send messages to their subscribers. All you need to know is the subscriber's phone number and carrier. Keep those carriers' pages bookmarked and use them to send text messages easily. Even if your phone *is* text-message capable, it pays to send messages from the Web, because by doing so you avoid messaging charges. See the end of this chapter for a list of some carriers that support Web-based texting.

## Text-based information services

Here's another way that text messages are changing our world. In the UNIX world (calm down, it's not that scary), there are several commands that UNIX geeks use to check on the status of various servers or programs running on those servers. One such command is called *ping*, which sends a message to a server to see if a response gets returned. How does ping relate to the über-cool world of text messaging? With text messaging, the same thing can be accomplished by using one of dozens of services: You send out a request, and the service will return some information to you. For instance, suppose that I send a particular service a simple text message containing a code and the letters AAPL. I am then sent a simple text message in reply, with the time

### SMS and Google

Internet giant Google now offers SMS users an easy way to *google* information on their phones. Surf on over to www.google.com/SMS to learn how to search the Web using SMS. (A special thanks to Amanda Jones for pointing this out.)

and the current stock-trading price of Apple Computer's stock. Using this method, I can "ping" financial data, sports information, headlines, horoscopes, and much more.

## Composing and Sending SMS Messages

Just when you thought you were relatively speedy at typing out those emails all day, along comes a new way of getting your message across. However, this is not like the kind of typing that you learned in the ninth grade. This is the new world, which requires a new way of thinking about text input. Humans always seem to seek the path of least resistance, and laboriously pecking out those lengthy text messages begged for some relief. So, along came the text acronym to the rescue. Now, text messaging can't claim all the glory for the rise of this new form of digital slang (or, as some claim, language butchery). To be fair, much of the credit goes to two-way pagers and the instant-messaging world. However, the rapid proliferation of texting has pushed the micro-language of acronyms to new complexity and popularity.

Now this new bastardized language isn't all bad. In fact its acronyms relieve you from laboriously typing out those long words and replaces them with much shorter words or numbers that, if read out loud, probably will sound the same, and end up getting the message across. Take a look at this chart and keep it handy when you text. Not only will it save you time and effort, but because most carriers limit the text messages you send or receive to 100 to 150 characters, it will also allow you to pack more information into a 10¢ message. However, even though you may feel very clever sending these cryptic messages, if the person on the other end isn't as cool as you (or is older than, say, 25 years old), he or she may have no idea what you're talking about.

# Commonly Used SMS Shorthand

| TEXT | TRANSLATION | TEXT | TRANSLATION |
|---|---|---|---|
| 1ce | once | cid | consider it done |
| 2 | to | cmi | call me |
| 2day | today | coz | because |
| 2moro | tomorrow | ctr | center |
| 2nite | tonight | cu | see you |
| 4 | for | cu @ | see you around |
| 911 | emergency, call me | cul or cul8tr | see you later |
| add | address | cuz | because |
| afaik | as far as i know | d, de, da | the |
| aka | also known as | don | doing |
| asap | as soon as possible | dylm | do you like me |
| atb | all the best | ez | easy |
| ayor | at your own risk | f2f | face to face |
| b | be | f2t | free to talk |
| b/c | because | fotflol | falling on the floor laughing out loud |
| b4 | before | fyi | for your information |
| b4n or bfn | bye for now | gal | get a life |
| bbl | be back late(r) | gr8 or grt | great |
| bcnu | be seeing you | gtg | got to go |
| b'day | birthday | gudluk | good luck |
| bhl8 | be home late | h8 | hate |
| bil | boss is listening | hak | hugs and kisses |
| brb | be right back | hand | have a nice day |
| btdt | been there done that | how r u | how are you |
| btw | by the way | ic | i see |
| buzz off | buzz off | iluvu | i love you |
| c | see | imho | in my humble opinion |

| TEXT | TRANSLATION |
| --- | --- |
| imnsho | in my not so humble opinion |
| imtng | in meeting |
| iyq | i like you |
| j/k or jk | kidding or just kidding |
| jic | just in case |
| k | okay |
| kit | keep in touch |
| kwim | know what i mean |
| l8 | late |
| l8er or l8r | later |
| lol | laughing out loud |
| luv or lv | love |
| mgmt | management |
| msg | message |
| mtfbwu | may the force be with you |
| mtg | meeting |
| mth | month |
| myob | mind your own business |
| n | and |
| n/a | not applicable |
| ne | any |
| ne1 | anyone |
| nethng | anything |
| no1 | no one |
| nufn | nothing |
| np | no problem |
| nvm | never mind |
| oic | oh, i see |

| TEXT | TRANSLATION |
| --- | --- |
| omg | oh, my god |
| pcm or pcme | please call me |
| pls or plz | please |
| ppl | people |
| r | are |
| rgds | regards |
| rtfm | read the flippin' manual |
| ru | are you |
| ru cmng | are you coming |
| ru ok or ruok | are you ok? |
| sit | stay in touch |
| spk | speak |
| stfu | shut the flip up |
| sum1 | someone |
| tel | telephone |
| thkq or tq | thank you |
| thx or tx | thanks |
| tmb | text me back |
| ttyl | talk to you later |
| txt bac | text back |
| tyvm | thank you very much |
| u | you |
| ur | your |
| ura* | you are a star |
| urqat | you are a cutie |
| w/ | with |
| w/o | without |
| w8 | wait |

| TEXT | TRANSLATION | | TEXT | TRANSLATION |
|------|-------------|--|------|-------------|
| w84m | wait for me | | wud? | what you doing |
| w8n | waiting | | x | kiss |
| wan2 | want to | | xlnt | excellent |
| wan2tlk | want to talk? | | xoxox | hugs and kisses |
| wknd | weekend | | y | why |
| wot | what | | yr | your |
| wru | where are you? | | yyssw | yeah yeah sure sure whatever |
| wu | what's up? | | | |

## SMS and MMS

Okay, now that your mind is sufficiently numb from thinking about all that text messaging has to offer, consider the new kid on the block: Multimedia Messaging Service (MMS). Think of it as *Text Trek: The Next Generation*. MMS picks up where text messaging left off— that is, if sending a text message is analogous to sending an email, then sending a MMS message would be like sending that same email with photos, video, or audio embedded in it. Basically, MMS is like sending a tiny PowerPoint presentation. An MMS message consists of one or more pages of photos combined with text and/or audio or video.

MMS messaging is becoming increasingly popular as camera phones take root. As they say, a picture is worth a thousand thumb-typed words. Describing a scene with text is harder than just sending a quick snapshot. MMS allows users to send images and audio with the immediacy of a phone call, but with the passivity of SMS—truly the best of both worlds. Picture this: I'm sitting on the beach in Maui and I decide to rub it in your face. Using my camera phone, I take a shot of the beautiful waves rolling in against an impossibly blue sky and then record myself saying something taunting like, "It's so beautiful here! Wish you were with me—not!" Once I hit *Send*, that MMS message with the photo and audio will pop up on your screen within minutes. Ah, glorious technology—bringing the art of bragging to new heights (or lows).

The catch here is that SMS is a mature technology, but MMS is still in its infancy. Many phones and carriers that easily support SMS do not yet support MMS, and those that do often charge extra for it. For example, AT&T Wireless charges 10¢ per SMS message, and 40¢ per MMS message. So, send those MMS messages with care. Also, even if you're one of the chosen few who has an MMS-capable phone, you may be speaking an alien tongue to the many more pedestrian SMS-capable mobile phones on the planet. Do yourself a favor and check with your recipients (via SMS?) to ensure they can receive your glorious MMS messages. Sore feet are the price you pay for dancing on the cutting edge.

## Major carrier text-messaging Web sites

**AT&T Wireless:** www.mymmode.com/messagecenter/init

**Cingular:** www.cingular.com/sendamessage

**Nextel:** www.nextel.com/services/mobilemessaging/index.shtml

**Sprint PCS:** http://messaging.sprintpcs.com/textmessaging/

**T-Mobile:** www.t-mobile.com/messaging/

**Verizon:** www.vtext.com/customer_site/jsp/messaging_lo.jsp

*Or, check sites that offer free text messaging around the globe, like:*

**Teleflip:** www.teleflip.com/

**TextMeFree:** www.textmefree.com/

# CHAPTER SEVEN

# Getting Online with Your Cell Phone

*It wasn't so long ago that we thought the world was just fine without laptops, the Internet, and mobile phones. Today, many jobs would be difficult or impossible without them. And now you can combine these devices together to make an instant, portable office.*

*Of course, the fastest way to access the Internet is with an Ethernet connection to a broadband service: The next best way to connect is through Wi-Fi. If neither of these options is available, your laptop's internal modem provides a somewhat reliable, albeit slow, way to get online— that is, if your ISP offers dial-up service, and you're near an analog phone line.*

*But what about when you're out in the middle of nowhere, and none of these traditional connection methods is available?*

Fortunately, the answer may be in the palm of your hand (or in your purse) in the form of your cell phone. With a little effort, it's possible to access the Internet through the virtually omnipresent cellular networks by using your cell phone as a modem. Your data-transfer speeds can be anywhere from as slow as dial-up to as fast as broadband, depending on your phone, service provider, and signal strength.

Connecting to the Internet through your mobile phone is a *last-resort* option. Your phone bill will be inflated (especially if data roaming charges apply), but it sure beats being cut off from the Internet entirely.

## Signing up for Data Service

The first thing you need to do is check with your cell phone service provider to see if your current phone is capable of being used as a data modem. Just because it can download ringtones and Web pages does not mean your phone has the horsepower to provide full Internet access to your laptop.

Once you have a data-capable phone, you need to add a data plan to your voice service. Prices for data plans range from $10 per month for minimal access to $80 for unlimited, all-you-can-eat data transfer. After signing up for a data plan, your mobile phone service provider also becomes your wireless ISP and will probably assign you a user-name, password, and Access Point Name (APN). I show you what to do with this information later in this chapter.

*You might need to upgrade your cell phone's firmware to properly handle data. Double-check with your service provider while you're signing up for data access; it can save you troubleshooting headaches down the line.*

# Connecting Your Cell Phone and Laptop

You connect a data-capable cell phone to a laptop computer either with a USB cable or wirelessly via infrared (IrDA) or Bluetooth. All three of these connection options are more than fast enough to handle current, real-world cellular data transfer speeds, so speed-wise it doesn't matter which one you use—the data transfer rate between your carrier and your phone is usually slower than that between your phone and your computer. There are other factors to consider, but the choice will probably be made for you based on which connection method your phone and laptop have in common.

## CDMA phones

If you have a CDMA cell phone (see the Phone Carriers chart in Chapter 1), you probably don't have Bluetooth—they tend to have USB and IrDA ports instead. Of the two non-Bluetooth options, USB is the way to go because it's easier to maintain a connection over an inexpensive (less than $30) data cable than it is over infrared. IrDA connections, because they need to stay aimed at each other, can be iffy at best. For example, maintaining an IrDA connection in a moving vehicle is a challenge.

Connecting a phone to a laptop via USB is a snap. You buy the correct data cable for the make and model of your phone (or, in some cases, you might have to buy a "connection kit" from your cell phone provider), then plug one end of the cable into the cell phone and the other end into an empty USB 1.1 or 2.0 port on your laptop. That's it.

## GSM phones

GSM phones, on the other hand, can be found sporting combinations of all three types of ports. If you have a choice, go with Bluetooth because it doesn't have the restrictions of the other two methods. Bluetooth doesn't require a cable as does USB, and its 30-foot range is much greater than the one-meter line-of-sight limitation of IrDA. However, not all mobile phones are Bluetooth phones. If you're not sure of your phone's capabilities, check its documentation or contact the phone's manufacturer.

## Laptops

Almost all current laptops have USB ports, which can be used either for cabling directly to a cell phone or adding on plug-in Bluetooth capabilities. In terms of cable-free connections, Bluetooth has largely superseded IrDA in recent years. If you're not sure of your laptop's capabilities, check its documentation, contact the manufacturer, or look for the official USB or Bluetooth symbols next to the computer's ports.

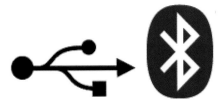

*USB ports are easily identifiable by their trident-like symbol (left), but not all Bluetooth devices bear the official Bluetooth symbol (right).*

# Connecting with Bluetooth

Like Wi-Fi, Bluetooth technology is also a radio-based, wireless technology. It was designed to replace the cables that many devices use to communicate with each other, but it actually wasn't meant to be used for the Internet because it operates at a much slower speed than Wi-Fi—0.721 megabits per second (Mbps) for Bluetooth versus 11 Mbps for 802.11b Wi-Fi—and it has a much shorter range: only 30 feet versus 150 feet for 802.11b.

Bluetooth replaces low-speed data cables the most effectively. For instance, some cell phones have replaced the wire connecting their headsets with wireless Bluetooth headsets. This way your phone can remain in your purse, briefcase, or pocket while you walk down the street seemingly having a conversation with your invisible friend. Bluetooth also works well with keyboards and mice because it easily handles the relatively small amount of data transferred between these input devices and a computer.

Bluetooth has become much more than just a cable-eliminating technology, however. It also allows "ad hoc" networking. Bluetooth-enabled laptops can become aware of each other when they get within a certain range, allowing you to set up your own Bluetooth network. If you came within radio range of a Bluetooth-enabled printer, suddenly your device has the ability to print! You could print from your mobile phone, laptop computer, or PDA. These ad hoc, temporary networking arrangements happen automatically once the devices have been paired, or authorized to access and utilize the services of each other. After pairing the devices, they will "automagically" handshake and work happily together as long as they are within wireless earshot of each other.

The most amazing use of Bluetooth, though, is turning your cell phone into your laptop's modem. But first, both devices have to have Bluetooth enabled.

## To check your laptop for Bluetooth capability

**Mac:** Choose Apple > System Preferences. If your computer has Bluetooth installed, its icon appears in the hardware row. If it doesn't, you will have to purchase an add-on Bluetooth device.

**Windows XP:** Choose Start > My Computer. Click the "View system information" link listed under System Tasks at left. In the System Properties window, click the Hardware tab. Click the Device Manager button. If your computer has Bluetooth installed, it may be listed as a network adapter or in the Bluetooth radios category.

*There are many different PC Card (PCMCIA) and USB adapters that can easily and inexpensively (less than $50) add Bluetooth capabilities to a laptop that doesn't already have it on board. Bluetooth adapters are also available for cell phones, but they allow you to connect to Bluetooth headsets only; you can't use them to connect to a Bluetooth-enabled computer.*

Connecting a phone to a laptop via Bluetooth is a little more involved than just plugging in a cable. *Pairing* is the term to describe the process of two devices getting to know each other—that is, allowing one to access the services of the other. For more specific information on how to pair your devices, you may need to consult the documentation that came with your phone and Bluetooth adapter.

## To pair a Bluetooth cell phone and laptop

*Warning! Leaving Bluetooth activated on your phone all the time is a potential security lapse that could be exploited by hackers, and leaving Bluetooth devices discoverable all the time makes it easier to gain unauthorized access to them.*

1. Activate the Bluetooth option on the cell phone. Bluetooth uses battery power, so it should be turned on only when needed.

2. Make your cell phone *visible* or *discoverable* by choosing the appropriate command (sometimes called Show Phone) in your phone's Bluetooth menu or the equivalent. This basically broadcasts the phone's availability to other Bluetooth devices (that happen to be listening) within range.

3. Turn on Bluetooth on your laptop. As with the cell phone, Bluetooth needs juice to operate, so turning it off when unused extends your battery life.

   - **Mac:** Choose Apple > System Preferences. Click Bluetooth. Click Turn Bluetooth On.

   - **Windows XP:** Depends on the driver provided by your Bluetooth adapter's vendor. Look in the Bluetooth Devices control panel or choose from the Bluetooth menu in the task tray.

4. Pair the cell phone with the laptop. Pairing authorizes the two devices to securely talk to one another. Once a Bluetooth pair is

created, it is remembered, and the process does not have to be repeated.

- **Mac:** In Bluetooth preferences, open the Devices pane. Click Set Up New Device to launch the Bluetooth Setup Assistant. Follow the on-screen instructions for setting up a mobile phone.

- **Windows XP:** In the Bluetooth Devices control panel, click Add. In the wizard that appears, select the "My device is set up and ready to be found" checkbox, then click Next. After a few seconds of scanning, your phone should appear in the list of Bluetooth devices discovered in range. Select the cell phone and click Next. Enter a passkey on the laptop and then enter the same passkey on the cell phone.

5. Turn off discoverability on your cell phone. This makes it harder for hackers to discover your phone, but does not affect the ability of paired devices to communicate with one another.

Once you have connected your laptop with your mobile phone via USB cable or Bluetooth, you can transfer data between them, allowing you to synchronize address books and calendars, for example. However, one of the real benefits for road warriors is the ability to use this connection to get online.

## Using your cell phone as a modem

You may be able to use your cell phone just as you would a traditional modem, dialing into your ISP's local access number. The main appeal of this option is that it is essentially free because it uses voice minutes from your cell phone service plan to access your existing ISP account. However, it is painfully slow (usually no faster than

 *Most phone manufacturers provide PC-only modem scripts. Mac users can find free scripts for many of the most common phones at www.taniwha.org.uk.*

*GPRS users will have many different scripts to choose from for any particular cell phone. First try the one with +CGQREQ in its name. It is also important that the script's Connected Information Device (CID) number match your cell phone's CID number (1 through 6). You may be able to find the CID by checking the data account information screen on your cell phone. If not, you will have to experiment by trying each script in turn until you find the one that works.*

14.4 kilobits per second) and unreliable. This option is largely being phased out and replaced by data-service plans.

These days, if you want to get online, the best solution is to subscribe to a data access plan from your mobile phone service provider. If you need to be online while on the road, the added cost is worthwhile because today's cellular networks offer fast and reliable data transmission.

When you signed up for data access, your cell phone service provider should have given you a connection kit with all the necessary account information and a modem script file for your particular phone model. If you didn't get a script, download the appropriate one from your phone manufacturer's Web site or search Google for the term *modem script* plus the make and model of your cell phone.

### TO SET UP BLUETOOTH DIAL-UP ACCESS ON A MACINTOSH

1. Copy your phone's modem script file into /Library/Modem Scripts.

2. Choose Apple > System Preferences. Click Network.

3. From the Show pop-up menu, choose the correct port to use.

   - If you're using a phone connected via a USB cable, the name of the phone should appear in the list.

   - If you're using a phone connected via Bluetooth, the port is called Bluetooth.

4. Click the Modem or Bluetooth Modem button.

*Mac OS X comes with scripts for many phones. If you've downloaded a modem script file and the Finder warns you that a file with that name already exists, don't replace it unless your copy is newer than the one already installed.*

Depending on your phone and service provider, you may need to change the default settings for the checkboxes and radio buttons in the Modem pane. Check the ReadMe file that came with your modem script.

5.   From the Modem pop-up menu, choose your mobile phone. (If you didn't properly install its script in step 1, it will not appear in this menu.)

6.   Click the PPP button, and (using the information provided by your cell phone company) fill in the Account Name, Password, and Telephone Number fields.

The Telephone Number field is filled in with either an APN or a General Packet Radio Service (GPRS) CID string. If you are entering an APN, it'll be alphanumeric, like a domain name. If you are entering a GPRS CID string, it'll be something like *99**2#.

7.   Click PPP Options and deselect the "Send PPP echo packets" checkbox.

8.   Click OK.

9.   Click Apply Now.

10.   Click Dial Now. The Internet Connect application launches.

11.   Click Connect. After a few seconds, your Internet connection should be established, and you will be able to use your Web browser, email client, and other Internet applications just as if you had a dial-up connection, only faster. When you are done, return to Internet Connect and click Disconnect.

**TO SET UP BLUETOOTH DIAL-UP ACCESS ON WINDOWS XP**

Your setup process will vary, depending on your service provider, phone, operating system software, and service plan. Contact your service provider for specific details on how to get online using your Windows laptop and your cell phone, and check www.fredjohnson. net/globalmobile for updates on using a Windows laptop with Bluetooth.

 *For additional advice on setting up Bluetooth on PCs, try searching the Microsoft site for your OS and devices (http://support.microsoft. com/) or Google for pages that address your particular needs.*

## Other Cellular Options

If connecting your laptop to your cell phone seems complicated, there are other alternatives to consider. You can buy a mid-range phone capable of surfing WAP sites and checking your email. Or get a full-fledged smart phone with full Internet support, including HTML, instant messaging, email, and so on. Smart phones are convenient because you don't have to lug around your laptop, but the small screen size and often-cumbersome data-input techniques may make this option impractical for some uses.

You can also skip the cell phone altogether and spring for a cellular card for your laptop, such as the Sierra Wireless AirCard. These credit-card sized devices plug directly into your laptop's PC Card (PCMCIA) slot and give you access to a cellular service provider's data network without the need for a separate cell phone.

CELL PHONES

# CHAPTER EIGHT

# Emerging Technologies

*After reading this book, you should be very well equipped to travel globally while continuing to be productive. But this book only represents a moment in time. Technology moves at such a rapid pace that there are some really compelling developments on the horizon poised to change the very way we communicate.*

# Cell Phone Trends

Cell-phone manufacturers are developing new and more advanced models of their handsets at a breakneck pace. Just a few years ago, people were thrilled by the notion of simply carrying a phone around with them. Just having a mobile phone was a status symbol—they were new, expensive, and kind of elitist. Today, pretty much everyone has a mobile phone, and even some young children carry around phones. And when I say "young" I mean under 12. It goes without saying that most, if not all, card-carrying teenagers already have their own cell phones and are, of course, masters of the text-messaging phenomenon.

Today's state-of-the-art mobile phones typically include fully functional calendars, address books, customizable ringtones, games, Web browsers, email clients, text messaging, digital cameras, and more. Tomorrow's phones will continue evolving and will offer these features and more. Although sub-megapixel, blurry images are the norm on today's camera phones (resulting in substandard photographs), there are phones slated for introduction over the next year with multi-megapixel digital cameras incorporated into their designs.

New features that allow you to share your photos over a wireless network and the Internet will also begin to emerge. Imagine taking a beautiful photo and posting it to your Web site or blog immediately from the comfort of your cell phone.

The evolution of the so-called *smart phone* is another story entirely. With the current state of today's wireless networks, phones have the ability to always be connected. This *always-on* feature is allowing phones to function as full-fledged Internet citizens. Your phone might soon have its own IP (Internet Protocol) address and will allow you to run Web server, instant messaging, or other Internet software from your pocket. Imagine—people from anywhere on the planet could potentially surf on over to your pocket to see the pages you've just posted.

The palmOne Treo 600 and the newly released Treo 650 already sport the ability to serve up Web pages (albeit with a little hacking). Expect this behavior to become more commonplace in the future.

Learn more about cell phones at:

http://inventors.about.com/library/weekly/aa070899.htm

## SIM Cards

We discussed the role of SIM cards earlier in this book, in Chapter 1. However, the role of the SIM card may be expanding even in the near future. Consider that the SIM card in your current GSM phone is basically a debit card connected to your account with whatever carrier you've chosen. Your SIM card contains account information and passwords and can even store contact information.

In Japan and Europe, some carriers are already experimenting with ways to let you pay for purchases via mobile phones. In some areas of Japan, for example, you can walk up to a vending machine, dial a phone number that correlates to your desired selection, and out comes your product. No cash changes hands, no muss, no fuss. Some experts have predicted that many purchases will occur this way in the future, including movie tickets, fast food, and public transportation. The SIM card paired with a private PIN could help pave the way to the cashless society that people have been dreaming of for years.

M-Systems, a major manufacturer of flash memory, is betting that hundreds of millions of SIM cards will be used in the coming years. To capitalize on the demand for newer and higher-capacity phones, they are building SIM cards capable of high-capacity data storage. These new SIM cards will enable Multimedia Messaging Service

(MMS), MP3 music, video clips, and high-resolution picture storage. The popularity and ubiquity of mobile phones, coupled with these types of advances, might signal the end of the need to carry other devices. However, one of the major hurdles that remains is battery life. With all of these capabilities, such as photography, music, data, purchases, and more, it's becoming increasingly critical that battery technology evolves to match our voracious usage.

Learn more about SIM cards at:

http://electronics.howstuffworks.com/cell-phone.htm

## Ringtones

The evolution of mobile phones and their increasingly sophisticated inner workings has given rise to the ringtones sub-industry. In the past, we were happy with just the customary ringing sound. Then, as time moved on and manufacturers introduced clever ringing sounds, it became in vogue to have an interesting ringtone on your phone. It's kind of like saying, "Look how cool I am," without actually saying it.

With the rapid rise in the popularity of digital music and the fact that phones are beginning to allow MP3 ringtones, a fledgling industry has sprung up—one that generated more than $1 billion by the end of 2004, according to Juniper Research. However, our love affair with ringtones may be waning; Juniper also forecasts that revenues will slowly decline to around $490 million by 2008.

Record labels have been quick to key in on this lucrative revenue stream. Consider that popular artists Eminem, Beyoncé, Jay-Z, and many more have all released tracks exclusively for ringtone use.

Learn more about ringtones at:

www.mobile1ringtones.com

### Ringback tones

*Ringback* tones take ringtones to a new level. You might not have realized it, but the ringing sound that you hear when you phone someone and are waiting for them to pick the phone up is yet another way to customize your mobile-phone experience (and for carriers to squeeze a few more dollars out of you).

Verizon Wireless recently announced it will be the first national carrier to offer ringback tones. These are short clips of real music that will replace the standard ring that callers hear when they call Verizon customers who have subscribed to the service. Customers in Sacramento and throughout southern California will be among the first to be able to personalize the sounds callers hear before a call is answered. Verizon says all of its customers will have access to the service by mid-2005. Options include a standard ringback tone (including the Verizon Wireless standard ringback tone)—or customers can choose to have different ringback tones play for different callers based on the Caller ID, user-specified group lists, or the time of day.

Learn more about ringback tones at:

http://vzwrbt.ztango.com

## VoIP

*Voice over Internet Protocol*, or VoIP, is the process of converting your voice into data that can then be transferred over the Internet to another computer, which then decodes that data back into audio. VoIP is poised to change the way we think about making calls, because by using your existing Internet connection, you can call anyone in the world with an Internet connection. Several services have sprouted up to make this process easier.

Vonage and Skype are just two of the many VoIP services that allow you to phone either other computer users or make Internet to POTS (Plain Old Telephone Service) calls—computer to phone. Once you've downloaded Skype's software, you can make free phone calls over the Internet to anyone else running the software. And for an additional fee (about 2¢ per minute) you can call anyone using a regular telephone.

Vonage is a similar company to Skype, but much more telco-like. Using its software, you can make calls over the Internet to other Vonage users. However, to take full advantage of the service, you need to install the free phone adapter, which allows you to keep your existing phone number and add as many additional phone numbers as you like in whatever area codes you desire. Vonage also has a software-only version called Vonage SoftPhone. This is a screen-based interface that works just like your telephone key-pad. You can make and receive calls and pick up your voicemail. SoftPhone also supports Caller ID and call forwarding.

Learn more about VoIP at:

www.skype.com *or* www.vonage.com

## Wi-Fi

The Wi-Fi phenomenon is taking the world by storm. Wireless hot-spots seem to be popping up everywhere—from coffee shops to bookstores to fast-food joints. Some enterprising cities such as Philadelphia have taken things a step further by deciding to blanket their entire city in Wi-Fi access—for free! Other cities are bringing broadband Internet access to their entire populations: Grand Haven, Michigan, is completely covered in wireless goodness, as are Athens,

Georgia, and Baltimore. Even Taipei has announced plans to cover the entire city in a wireless cloud.

Once Wi-Fi is everywhere, the road will be paved for other Wi-Fi-dependent devices. Currently in development are VoIP-enabled Wi-Fi cell phones. These phones will enable you to not only bypass the traditional phone company, but also bypass your wireless carrier for the much cheaper VoIP rates. Streaming radio receivers could be built into cars to allow Internet radio anytime, anywhere. Sirius Radio, are you listening?

Learn more about Wi-Fi at:

http://computer.howstuffworks.com/wireless-network.htm

## Personal Ad Hoc Networks

Bluetooth technology isn't just for hooking up devices. Some enterprising entrepreneurs have cooked up a way to allow you to form personal ad hoc networks. They've devised a way for you to hook up with that special someone, all through the magic of Bluetooth wireless technology.

A few services out there are betting on Bluetooth to be the world's best high-tech ice-breaker. One such company is ProxiDating.com: The company has created software that you can install on your cell phone, and when you come within striking range of your potential date (striking range is about 50 feet), assuming that person is signed up with the same service, both of your phones will alert you. ProxiDating automatically will send the text and the picture you've defined to the other person and, likewise, you'll receive his or her text and picture. Then it's up to you to move in with your best Bluetooth line. "Say, that's a really nice phone…."

# GSM Frequencies, Country by Country

*Different countries use different GSM frequencies. If you have a three-band mobile phone, you should be able to use it in numerous countries around the globe. All you need to do is switch your phone to the correct band and you'll pick up a signal within minutes. The following is a list of GSM frequencies used by each country to help you plan your gear accordingly.*

| COUNTRY | GSM FREQUENCIES | COUNTRY | GSM FREQUENCIES |
|---|---|---|---|
| Afghanistan | (GSM 900/1800) | Bermuda | (GSM 1900) |
| Albania | (GSM 900/1800) | Bolivia | (GSM 1900) |
| Algeria | (GSM 900/1800) | Bosnia-Herzegovina | (GSM 900) |
| American Samoa | (GSM 1900) | Botswana | (GSM 900) |
| Andorra | (GSM 900) | Brazil | (GSM 1800) |
| Angola | (GSM 900) | Brunei Darussalam | (GSM 900) |
| Antigua & Barbuda | (GSM 1900) | Bulgaria | (GSM 900/1800) |
| Argentina | (GSM 900/1900) | Burkina Faso | (GSM 900) |
| Armenia | (GSM 900) | Burundi | (GSM 900) |
| Aruba | (GSM 900/1800/1900) | Cambodia | (GSM 900) |
| Australia | (GSM 900/1800/3G) | Cameroon | (GSM 900) |
| Austria | (GSM 900/1800/3G) | Canada | (GSM 1900) |
| Azerbaijan | (GSM 900) | Cape Verde Island | (GSM 900) |
| Bahrain | (GSM 900) | Central African Republic | (GSM 900) |
| Bangladesh | (GSM 900) | Chad | (GSM 900) |
| Belarus | (GSM 900) | Chile | (GSM 1900) |
| Belgium | (GSM 900/1800) | China | (GSM 900) |
| Belize | (GSM 1900) | Congo | (GSM 900) |
| Benin | (GSM 900) | Costa Rica | (GSM 1800/3G) |

| COUNTRY | GSM FREQUENCIES | COUNTRY | GSM FREQUENCIES |
|---|---|---|---|
| Cote d'Ivoire | (GSM 900) | Gambia | (GSM 900) |
| Croatia | (GSM 900) | Georgia | (GSM 900/1800) |
| Cuba | (GSM 900) | Germany | (GSM 900/1800/3G) |
| Cyprus | (GSM 900) | Ghana | (GSM 900) |
| Czech Republic | (GSM 900/1800) | Gibraltar | (GSM 900) |
| Denmark | (GSM 900/1800) | Greece | (GSM 900/1800) |
| Dominican Republic | (GSM 1900) | Greenland | (GSM 900) |
| Egypt | (GSM 900) | Grenada | (GSM 900) |
| El Salvador | (GSM 900) | Guam (USA) | (GSM 1900) |
| Equatorial Guinea | (GSM 900/1800) | Guernsey | (GSM 900) |
| Estonia | (GSM 900/1800) | Guinea | (GSM 900) |
| Ethiopia | (GSM 900) | Honduras | (GSM 1900) |
| Faeroe Islands | (GSM 900) | Hong Kong | (GSM 900/1800) |
| Fiji Islands | (GSM 900) | Hungary | (GSM 900/1800) |
| Finland | (GSM 900/1800) | Iceland | (GSM 900/1800) |
| France | (GSM 900/1800) | India | (GSM 900/1800) |
| French Polynesia | (GSM 900) | Indonesia | (GSM 900/1800) |
| French West Indies | (GSM 900/1800) | Iran | (GSM 900) |
| Gabon | (GSM 900) | Iraq | (GSM 900/1800) |

| COUNTRY | GSM FREQUENCIES | COUNTRY | GSM FREQUENCIES |
|---|---|---|---|
| Ireland | (GSM 900/1800) | Lithuania | (GSM 900/1800) |
| Isle of Man | (GSM 900/1800) | Luxembourg | (GSM 900/1800) |
| Israel | (GSM 900/1800/3G) | Macau | (GSM 900/1800) |
| Italy | (GSM 900/1800/3G) | Macedonia | (GSM 900) |
| Jamaica | (GSM 900) | Madagascar | (GSM 900/1800) |
| Japan | (GSM 3G) | Malawi | (GSM 900) |
| Jersey | (GSM 900) | Malaysia | (GSM 900/1800) |
| Jordan | (GSM 900) | Maldives | (GSM 900/1800) |
| Kazakhstan | (GSM 900) | Mali | (GSM 900) |
| Kenya | (GSM 900) | Malta | (GSM 900/1800) |
| Kuwait | (GSM 900/1800) | Mauritania | (GSM 900) |
| Kyrgyzstan | (GSM 900) | Mauritius | (GSM 900) |
| Laos | (GSM 900) | Mexico | (GSM 1900) |
| Latvia | (GSM 900/1800) | Micronesia | (GSM 900) |
| Lebanon | (GSM 900/1800) | Moldova | (GSM 900) |
| Lesotho | (GSM 900) | Monaco | (GSM 900) |
| Liberia | (GSM 900) | Mongolia | (GSM 900/1800) |
| Libya | (GSM 900) | Morocco | (GSM 900) |
| Liechtenstein | (GSM 900/1800) | Mozambique | (GSM 900/1800) |

| COUNTRY | GSM FREQUENCIES | COUNTRY | GSM FREQUENCIES |
|---------|-----------------|---------|-----------------|
| Myanmar | (GSM 900) | Poland | (GSM 900/1800) |
| Namibia | (GSM 900/1800) | Portugal | (GSM 900/1800/3G) |
| Nepal | (GSM 900) | Puerto Rico | (GSM 1900) |
| Netherlands | (GSM 900/1800) | Qatar | (GSM 900) |
| Netherlands Antilles | (GSM 900/1900) | Reunion Island | (GSM 900/1800) |
| New Caledonia | (GSM 900) | Romania | (GSM 900/1800) |
| New Zealand | (GSM 900) | Russia | (GSM 900/1800) |
| Nicaragua | (GSM 1900) | Rwanda | (GSM 900) |
| Niger | (GSM 900) | Sao Tome and Principe | (GSM 900) |
| Nigeria | (GSM 900/1800) | Saudi Arabia | (GSM 900) |
| Norway | (GSM 900/1800) | Senegal | (GSM 900) |
| Oman | (GSM 900) | Seychelles | (GSM 900) |
| Pakistan | (GSM 900) | Sierra Leone | (GSM 900) |
| Palestine | (GSM 900) | Singapore | (GSM 900/1800) |
| Panama | (GSM 900) | Slovakia | GSM 900/1800) |
| Papua New Guinea | (GSM 900) | Somalia | (GSM 900/1800) |
| Paraguay | (GSM 1900) | South Africa | (GSM 900/1800) |
| Peru | (GSM 1900) | South Korea | (GSM 3G) |
| Philippines | (GSM 900/1800) | Spain | (GSM 900/1800) |

| COUNTRY | GSM FREQUENCIES | COUNTRY | GSM FREQUENCIES |
|---|---|---|---|
| Sri Lanka | (GSM 900) | Turkmenistan | (GSM 900) |
| Sudan | (GSM 900) | Uganda | (GSM 900/1800) |
| Suriname | (GSM 900) | Ukraine | (GSM 900/1800) |
| Swaziland | (GSM 900) | United Arab Emirates | (GSM 900) |
| Sweden | (GSM 900/1800/3G) | United Kingdom | (GSM 900/1800/3G) |
| Switzerland | (GSM 900/1800) | Uruguay | (GSM 1800) |
| Syria | (GSM 900/1800) | USA | (GSM 1900) |
| Taiwan | (GSM 900/1800) | Uzbekistan | (GSM 900/1800) |
| Tajikistan | (GSM 900/1800) | Vanuatu | (GSM 900) |
| Tanzania | (GSM 900/1800/400) | Venezuela | (GSM 900/1800) |
| Thailand | (GSM 900/1800/1900/3G) | Vietnam | (GSM 900) |
| Togo | (GSM 900) | Virgin Islands | (GSM 900/1800) |
| Tonga | (GSM 900) | Yemen | (GSM 900) |
| Trinidad and Tobago | (GSM 1800) | Yugoslavia | GSM 900/1800 |
| Tunisia | (GSM 900) | Zambia | (GSM 900) |
| Turkey | (GSM 900/1800) | Zimbabwe | (GSM 900) |

# APPENDIX B

# Country Codes and International Access Numbers

To make a phone call to another country, you'll need to dial some additional numbers before you can dial the local number that you want to reach.

The first number is the *international access number* for the country that you're placing the call from. This number is essential because otherwise, your call will not be recognized as an overseas phone number. Many countries that share a geographic region use the same international access number—some of the most common are 00 and 011.

The second number that you need to dial is the *country code* of the destination for your call. Most countries have their own unique number, with a few exceptions—for example, the United States and Canada both share a country code of "1."

Once you've dialed these numbers, you can now key in the number of the person or business that you want to reach. In some countries, there might be additional area codes or city codes for regions within that country. Most likely, you already have these included in the number you're going to dial. And finally, some locales might list their phone number with an extra digit in front of it (such as a "0" in some European countries) that's meant for local dialing, but that extra digit might get dropped when phoning from outside the country.

For example, if you're in the United States and dialing a number in Amsterdam, you would first dial "011" for international access, then "31" for the Netherlands, and then the local number in Amsterdam, which would most likely begin with the Amsterdam regional code of "20." A good Web site to use as a reference for dialing information anywhere in the world is www.countrycallingcodes.com.

 *When you see a "~" in the international access code, this means that you must wait for a second tone at this stage before continuing to dial.*

| COUNTRY | COUNTRY CODE<br>(DIALING IN FROM ANOTHER COUNTRY) | INT'L ACCESS<br>(DIALING OUT TO ANOTHER COUNTRY) |
|---|---|---|
| Afghanistan | 93 | 00 |
| Albania | 355 | 00 |
| Algeria | 213 | 00 |
| American Samoa | 684 | 00 |
| Andorra | 376 | 00 |
| Angola | 244 | 00 |
| Anguilla | 264 | 011 |
| Antarctica | 672 | n/a |
| Antigua | 268 | 011 |
| Argentina | 54 | 00 |
| Armenia | 374 | 00 |
| Aruba | 297 | 00 |
| Ascension Island | 247 | 01 |
| Australia | 61 | 0011 |
| Austria | 43 | 00 |
| Azerbaijan | 994 | 8~10 |
| Bahamas | 242 | 001 |
| Bahrain | 973 | 0 |

| COUNTRY | COUNTRY CODE<br>(DIALING IN FROM ANOTHER COUNTRY) | INT'L ACCESS<br>(DIALING OUT TO ANOTHER COUNTRY) |
|---|---|---|
| Bangladesh | 880 | 00 |
| Barbados | 246 | 011 |
| Barbuda | 268 | 011 |
| Belarus | 375 | 8~10 |
| Belgium | 32 | 00 |
| Belize | 501 | 00 |
| Benin | 229 | 00 |
| Bermuda | 441 | 011 |
| Bhutan | 975 | 00 |
| Bolivia | 591 | 00 |
| Bosnia-Herzegovina | 387 | 00 |
| Botswana | 267 | 00 |
| Brazil | 55 | 00 |
| British Virgin Islands | 284 | 011 |
| Brunei Darussalam | 673 | 00 |
| Bulgaria | 359 | 00 |
| Burkina Faso | 226 | 00 |
| Burma (Myanmar) | 95 | 0 |

| COUNTRY | COUNTRY CODE (DIALING IN FROM ANOTHER COUNTRY) | INT'L ACCESS (DIALING OUT TO ANOTHER COUNTRY) |
|---|---|---|
| Burundi | 257 | 90 |
| Cambodia | 855 | 00 |
| Cameroon | 237 | 00 |
| Canada | 1 | 011 |
| Cape Verde Island | 238 | 0 |
| Cayman Islands | 345 | 011 |
| Central African Republic | 236 | 19 |
| Chad | 235 | 15 |
| Chile | 56 | 00 |
| China | 86 | 00 |
| Christmas Island | 61 | 00 |
| Cocos Islands | 61 | 0011 |
| Colombia | 57 | 90 |
| Comoros | 269 | 10 |
| Congo | 242 | 00 |
| Congo, Dem. Republic | 243 | 00 |
| Cook Islands | 682 | 00 |
| Costa Rica | 506 | 00 |

| COUNTRY | COUNTRY CODE (DIALING IN FROM ANOTHER COUNTRY) | INT'L ACCESS (DIALING OUT TO ANOTHER COUNTRY) |
|---|---|---|
| Croatia | 385 | 00 |
| Cuba | 53 | 119 |
| Curaçao | 599 | 00 |
| Cyprus | 357 | 00 |
| Czech Republic | 420 | 00 |
| Denmark | 45 | 00 |
| Diego Garcia | 246 | 00 |
| Djibouti | 253 | 00 |
| Dominica | 767 | 011 |
| Dominican Republic | 809 | 011 |
| Ecuador | 593 | 00 |
| Egypt | 20 | 00 |
| El Salvador | 503 | 0 |
| Equatorial Guinea | 240 | 00 |
| Eritrea | 291 | 00 |
| Estonia | 472 | 8~00 |
| Ethiopia | 251 | 00 |
| Faeroe Islands | 298 | 009 |

| COUNTRY | COUNTRY CODE (DIALING IN FROM ANOTHER COUNTRY) | INT'L ACCESS (DIALING OUT TO ANOTHER COUNTRY) |
|---------|-----------------------------------------------|-----------------------------------------------|
| Falkland Islands | 500 | 0 |
| Fiji Islands | 679 | 05 |
| Finland | 358 | 00 |
| France | 33 | 00 |
| French Antilles | 596 | 00 |
| French Guiana | 594 | 00 |
| French Polynesia | 689 | 00 |
| Gabon | 241 | 00 |
| Gambia | 220 | 00 |
| Georgia | 995 | 8~10 |
| Germany | 49 | 00 |
| Ghana | 223 | 00 |
| Gibraltar | 350 | 00 |
| Greece | 30 | 00 |
| Greenland | 299 | 009 |
| Grenada | 473 | 011 |
| Guadeloupe | 590 | 00 |
| Guam | 671 | 011 |

| COUNTRY | COUNTRY CODE<br>(DIALING IN FROM ANOTHER COUNTRY) | INT'L ACCESS<br>(DIALING OUT TO ANOTHER COUNTRY) |
|---|---|---|
| Guantanamo Bay | 5399 | 00 |
| Guatemala | 502 | 00 |
| Guernsey | 44 | 00 |
| Guinea | 224 | 00 |
| Guinea-Bissau | 245 | 00 |
| Guyana | 592 | 001 |
| Haiti | 509 | 00 |
| Honduras | 504 | 00 |
| Hong Kong | 852 | 001 |
| Hungary | 36 | 00 |
| Iceland | 354 | 00 |
| India | 91 | 00 |
| Indonesia | 62 | 001, 008 |
| Iran | 98 | 00 |
| Iraq | 964 | 00 |
| Ireland | 353 | 00 |
| Isle of Man | 44 | 00 |
| Israel | 972 | 00 |

| COUNTRY | COUNTRY CODE (DIALING IN FROM ANOTHER COUNTRY) | INT'L ACCESS (DIALING OUT TO ANOTHER COUNTRY) |
|---|---|---|
| Italy | 39 | 00 |
| Ivory Coast | 225 | 00 |
| Jamaica | 876 | 011 |
| Japan | 81 | 001 |
| Jordan | 962 | 00 |
| Kazakhstan | 7 | 8~10 |
| Kenya | 254 | 000 |
| Kiribati | 686 | 00 |
| Korea, North | 850 | 00 |
| Korea, South | 82 | 001 |
| Kuwait | 965 | 00 |
| Kyrgyzstan | 996 | 8~10 |
| Laos | 856 | 14 |
| Latvia | 371 | 00 |
| Lebanon | 961 | 00 |
| Lesotho | 266 | 00 |
| Liberia | 231 | 00 |
| Libya | 218 | 00 |

| COUNTRY | COUNTRY CODE (DIALING IN FROM ANOTHER COUNTRY) | INT'L ACCESS (DIALING OUT TO ANOTHER COUNTRY) |
|---|---|---|
| Liechtenstein | 423 | 00 |
| Lithuania | 370 | 8~10 |
| Luxembourg | 352 | 00 |
| Macau | 853 | 00 |
| Macedonia | 389 | 00 |
| Madagascar | 261 | 00 |
| Malawi | 265 | 101 |
| Malaysia | 60 | 00 |
| Maldives | 960 | 00 |
| Mali | 223 | 00 |
| Malta | 356 | 00 |
| Mariana Islands | 670 | 011 |
| Marshall Islands | 692 | 01110 |
| Martinique | 596 | 00 |
| Mauritania | 222 | 00 |
| Mauritius | 230 | 00 |
| Mayotte Island | 269 | 10 |
| Mexico | 52 | 00 |

| COUNTRY | COUNTRY CODE<br>(DIALING IN FROM ANOTHER COUNTRY) | INT'L ACCESS<br>(DIALING OUT TO ANOTHER COUNTRY) |
|---|---|---|
| Micronesia | 691 | 011 |
| Midway Island | 808 | 00 |
| Moldova | 272 | 8~10 |
| Monaco | 377 | 00 |
| Mongolia | 976 | 00 |
| Montserrat | 66 | 011 |
| Morocco | 212 | 00~ |
| Mozambique | 258 | 00 |
| Myanmar (Burma) | 95 | 0 |
| Namibia | 264 | 09 |
| Nauru | 674 | 00 |
| Nepal | 977 | 00 |
| Netherlands | 31 | 00 |
| Netherlands Antilles | 599 | 00 |
| Nevis | 869 | 011 |
| New Caledonia | 687 | 00 |
| New Zealand | 64 | 00 |
| Nicaragua | 505 | 00 |

| COUNTRY | COUNTRY CODE (DIALING IN FROM ANOTHER COUNTRY) | INT'L ACCESS (DIALING OUT TO ANOTHER COUNTRY) |
|---|---|---|
| Niger | 227 | 00 |
| Nigeria | 234 | 009 |
| Niue | 683 | 00 |
| Norfolk Island | 672 | 00 |
| Norway | 47 | 00 |
| Oman | 968 | 00 |
| Pakistan | 92 | 00 |
| Palau | 680 | 11 |
| Palestine | 970 | 00 |
| Panama | 507 | 0 |
| Papua New Guinea | 675 | 05 |
| Paraguay | 595 | 00 |
| Peru | 51 | 00 |
| Philippines | 63 | 00 |
| Poland | 48 | 0~0 |
| Portugal | 351 | 00 |
| Puerto Rico | 787 | 1 |
| Qatar | 974 | 0 |

| COUNTRY | COUNTRY CODE (DIALING IN FROM ANOTHER COUNTRY) | INT'L ACCESS (DIALING OUT TO ANOTHER COUNTRY) |
|---|---|---|
| Reunion Island | 262 | 00 |
| Romania | 40 | 00 |
| Russia | 7 | 8~10 |
| Rwanda | 250 | 00 |
| St. Helena | 290 | 01 |
| St. Kitts | 869 | 011 |
| St. Pierre & Miquelon | 508 | 00 |
| St. Vincent | 784 | 011 |
| San Marino | 378 | 00 |
| Sao Tome & Principe | 239 | 00 |
| Saudi Arabia | 966 | 00 |
| Senegal | 221 | 00 |
| Serbia | 381 | 00 |
| Seychelles | 248 | 00 |
| Sierra Leone | 232 | 00 |
| Singapore | 65 | 001 |
| Slovakia | 421 | 00 |
| Slovenia | 386 | 00 |

| COUNTRY | COUNTRY CODE (DIALING IN FROM ANOTHER COUNTRY) | INT'L ACCESS (DIALING OUT TO ANOTHER COUNTRY) |
|---|---|---|
| Solomon Islands | 677 | 00 |
| Somalia | 252 | 19 |
| South Africa | 27 | 09 or 091 |
| Spain | 34 | 00 |
| Sri Lanka | 94 | 00 |
| Sudan | 249 | 00 |
| Suriname | 597 | 00 |
| Swaziland | 268 | 00 |
| Sweden | 46 | 00 |
| Switzerland | 41 | 00 |
| Syria | 963 | 00 |
| Taiwan | 886 | 002 |
| Tajikistan | 992 | 8~10 |
| Tanzania | 255 | 00 |
| Thailand | 66 | 001 |
| Togo | 228 | 00 |
| Tonga | 676 | 00 |
| Trinidad & Tobago | 868 | 011 |

| COUNTRY | COUNTRY CODE (DIALING IN FROM ANOTHER COUNTRY) | INT'L ACCESS (DIALING OUT TO ANOTHER COUNTRY) |
|---|---|---|
| Tunisia | 216 | 00 |
| Turkey | 90 | 00 |
| Turkmenistan | 993 | 8~10 |
| Turks & Caicos | 649 | 011 |
| Tuvalu | 688 | 00 |
| Uganda | 256 | 00 |
| Ukraine | 380 | 8~10 |
| United Arab Emirates | 971 | 00 |
| United Kingdom | 44 | 00 |
| Uruguay | 598 | 00 |
| USA | 1 | 011 |
| Uzbekistan | 998 | 8~10 |
| Vanuatu | 678 | 00 |
| Vatican City | 39 | 00 |
| Venezuela | 58 | 00 |
| Vietnam | 84 | 00 |
| Virgin Islands | 1 | 011 |
| Wake Island | 808 | 00 |

| COUNTRY | COUNTRY CODE<br>(DIALING IN FROM ANOTHER COUNTRY) | INT'L ACCESS<br>(DIALING OUT TO ANOTHER COUNTRY) |
| --- | --- | --- |
| Wallis & Futuna | 681 | 19~ |
| Western Samoa | 685 | 0 |
| Yemen | 967 | 00 |
| Yugoslavia | 381 | 99 |
| Zambia | 260 | 00 |
| Zimbabwe | 263 | 00 |

# Index

INDEX

# Visit Peachpit on the Web at www.peachpit.com

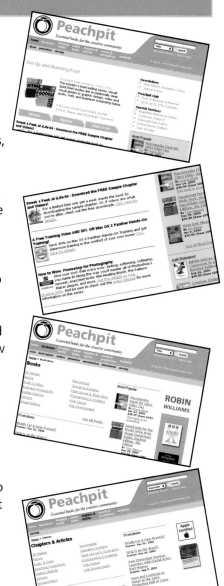

- Read the latest articles and download timesaving tipsheets from best-selling authors such as Scott Kelby, Robin Williams, Lynda Weinman, Ted Landau, and more!

- Join the Peachpit Club and save 25% off all your online purchases at peachpit.com every time you shop—plus enjoy free UPS ground shipping within the United States.

- Search through our entire collection of new and upcoming titles by author, ISBN, title, or topic. There's no easier way to find just the book you need.

- Sign up for newsletters offering special Peachpit savings and new book announcements so you're always the first to know about our newest books and killer deals.

- Did you know that Peachpit also publishes books by Apple, New Riders, Adobe Press, Macromedia Press, palmOne Press, and TechTV press? Swing by the Peachpit family section of the site and learn about all our partners and series.

- Got a great idea for a book? Check out our About section to find out how to submit a proposal. You could write our next best-seller!

**You'll find all this and more at www.peachpit.com.**
**Stop by and take a look today!**